Problems
of
Child Labour in India

Problems of Child Labour in India

Edited by :
Dr. R.N. Misra

Commonwealth

Problems of Child Labour in India

Ist Edition : 2004
ISBN 81-7169-835-2

Published by :
Ajay Verma
For Commonwealth Publishers
4831/24, Prahlad Street,
Ansari Road, Darya Ganj,
New Delhi - 110002
Phone : 23272541, 23257835
Fax: 91-011-23257835
E-mail : campusbooks@hotmail.com

Laser Typesetting by :
Stylish Laser Typesetter
Delhi

Printed at :
Roshan Offset Printers
Delhi

Introduction

The problem of Child Labour is very old. The child labour as a mode of exploitation was necessitated by the economic compulsion of the parents and the child himself. Though, child labour is a global problem, it has become a serious problem in developing countries like India. In India 40 per cent of population are children, out of this 25 per cent are engaged as child labourer. Poverty, illiteracy, unemployment, social customs, population explosion, low income of parents are major problems which forced a grown up child to work as labourer. Though, we have completed Ninth Plans, the standard of living of the people are not increasing upto the mark. So the problem of child labours is still in dark.

This book is of immense use, it throws light on various aspects on the problem of child labour in our country. This book will be very helpful to the planners, teachers research scholars, government, various non-government agencies who are thinking about the development of the notion as a whole.

Dr. R.N. Misra

Acknowledgement

I am very much thankful to all paper contributors, specially to Prof S.N. Jena, and Prof. N.P. Patro. All the paper contributors have touched various aspects of the problems of child labour in our country.

I am thankful to my wife Smt. Swarana Misra, who has helped and co-operated with me from various aspects for editing this book. I am also thankful to my sons Roopesh Kumar and Rookesh Kumar who have helped me as and when required to edit this book. Their love, affection co-operation has inspired me in editing this book.

I am also thankful to my friends Sri P.B. Patro, Sri G.R.G. Rao and Dr. Pitambar Dash and all other friends relatives and others who have helped me during the period of editing this book.

I am very much thankful and grateful to Sri B.R. Verma, of Commonwealth Publishers, New Delhi, who had readily accepted my proposal in publishing this book in spite of their heavy pressure during this session. I am also thankful to all the staff of Commonwealth Publishers, New Delhi, for their help and co-operation in publication of this book in time.

Dr. R.N. Misra

Contents

Contributors

Prof. Surendranath Jena was Born in 1922. He has passed M.Com. in the year 1948. He joined as a Lecturer in Commerce in the same year at G.M. College, Sambalpur. He joined as a Professor in Commerce at Khallikote College, Berhampur, in the year 1972, and retired from the service in the year 1980. He has presented a number of papers at National Level as well as State Levels Seminars.

Dr. Narsing Prasad Patro, born in 1935, has joined as a Lecturer in Economics in the year 1959 and continued till his retirement in 1993 as Professor of Economics. He has presented a number of papers at National Seminars. He has produced many Ph.D. Scholars.

Smt. Babilata Shroff, born in 27.03.1965, did her M.A. (Eco.) in the year 1986 from Berhampur University. At present she is working as a Lecturer in Economics at D.A.V. College, Titilagarh, Orissa. She has published eight articles.

Sri Roopesh Kumar Misra, born in May 1974, did his B.Sc. LL.B. From Berhampur University, MBA from Madras, and MCA from IGNOU, New Delhi. He has published six articles. At present he is a researched scholar.

Sri Baidyanath Dalai, born in April, 1959, did his M.Com. in 1982. He joined as a Lecturer in 1983. At present he is working at B.J.B. College, Bhubaneswar. Now he is doing his Ph.D. work under the guidance of Dr. R.N. Misra. He has published 10 articles.

Sri R.L. Panigrahy, born in July 1975, did his M.A. (Eco.) and PGDCA and 'B' Level MCA. He has published Four Books and two books are under press. He has also published 10 articles in different Journals. He is associated with different associations of India and Orissa.

Sri Kedar N. Bisoyee, did his M.A. (Pol. Sc.) from Berhampur University. After Working for 16 years as Lecturer, he joined as Project Director, at National Child Labour Project, under the Ministry of Labour, Government of India at Malkangiri, Orissa. He had submitted his thesis for Ph.D. Degree.

Sundarsan Jena, did his M.A. (Eco.) from Berhampur University. He has put up 21 years of service of teaching. AT present he is working as a Lecturer in Economics at Adivasi College, Balliguda, Orissa.

Md. Inshadun Nabi, did his P.G. in IRPM from Berhampur University. He is associated with number of social orgnisations.

Dr. S.N. Tripathy has 25 years of teaching experience. He has published eight books and produced 3 Ph.D. Scholars. At present he is working at Sc. College, Aska, Orissa.

B.C. Mahapatra is a retired Divisional Telecom Engineer. He is a good writer as well as a poet. Since his retirement he is actively engaged in social activities. He has taken various steps for the eradication of child labour in the district of Ganjam (Orissa).

Prof (Dr.) R.P. Sharma, a retired professor of Economics of Berhampur University. He was retired from his service in the year 1996. So far, he has produced eight Ph.D. scholars. At present he is the Director of the Institute of Economics Studies, Berhampur-10. He is associated with a good number of both academic and social organisations.

Dr. Mrityunjaya Mishra (b. 1962) did his M.A., M. Phil. from Berhampur University. He did his Ph.D. on Economics of Industrial Pollution in 1999 from the Berhampur University. Further, he did his post doctoral research study at Environment Department, University of York, U.K. He has visited Seven countries and attended Five International Seminars. At present he is working as Lecturer in Economics at Science College, Hinjilicut (Orissa).

Dr. D. Tata Rao (b. 1961) has passed his M. Com. from Andhra

University in 1983, B.Ed. in 1987 and M.Ed. in 1990. He did his Ph.D. work on Rural Artisans of Ganjam district of Orissa State in the year 2003. He has, so far, published five research articles in various journals. At present he is working as a Senior Lecturer in Commerce at Government Degree College, Ichchapuram under Andhra University.

Dr. S.N. Tripathy (b. 1957) is a renowned researcher and an author of more than ten books. He has successfully completed many a project funded by ICSSR and UGC. He has produced three Ph.D. scholars and is at present associated with the department of Economics, Aska Science College, Aska in the State of Orissa.

Sri G. Rajgopal Rao (b. 1951) has passed his M.Com. in the year 1974 from Berhampur University and joined in Government service in the year 1975 as lecturer in Commerce. He has published two books and eight articles in different journals. He has submitted his Ph.D. thesis on Rural Banks in Orissa, during 2002 to the Berhampur University. At present he is working as a faculty member of the department of Commerce at Government Autonomous College, Bhawanipatna in the State of Orissa.

1

Child Labour in the Global Era—A New Perspective

*—N.P. Patro**

(Recognised for long as a social evil, the practice of child labour for economic gain existed in nearly all countries at some time or the other. While the advanced countries are now much more free of this malaise, their developing counterparts experience a pressing need to tackle this issue which has assumed a complex nature. Looked at in the light of the process of globalisation which is on in these countries the issue becomes very intricate and requires a judiciously selected approach, what with the need for social justice and economic expediency.

This paper undertakes to examine the new dimension given to the issue of child labour in India by Globalisation and the concomitant processes of Liberalisation and Privatisation which work in unison as a package. Put in the right order of their arrangement these are known as LPG (*e.g.* Liberalisation, Privatisation and Globalisation). This study is conducted with the history, causes and nature of child labour in India forming the back drop which is taken up in Part-I).

PART I

In this broad, undifferentiated sense, child labour existed in India in all ages. In the ancient times the accepted principle was that every child worked with parents both at home and the work place. The parents, no doubt, had to be take proper care of the education of the child, whether male or female.

*Dr. N.P. Patro, is a retired Professor of Economics.

Bonded labour was prohibited. Occupations and professions being hereditary and caste-determined, such work gave the children the necessary preparations to face life when they come of age. Much the same practice continued till the advent of British Rule. The imposition of the British legal system, a specifically designed educational system and other practices meant to serve the British interest produced far-reaching effects on the people and society in India. The transfer of village lands to outsiders through sale broke the isolation and self-contained nature of the villages. It led to the creation of a new class of land-less agricultural labourers who, through time, drifted from rural to urban areas by economic necessity. The rise of the factory system in the mid-nineteenth century opened up avenues for employment of children of the vulnerable sections in factories and other work places. The children were forced to work in very harsh working conditions. Due to long working hours, harsh working conditions and very low wages most children had burnt themselves out by the time they came of adult-hood.

It is widely recognised now that child labour as a mode of exploitation was necessitated by the economic compulsions of the parents and the child himself. It is keeping these two aspects of the issue in view that V.V. Giri tended to call child labour as an economic necessity but a social evil. Depending upon the context, 'Child labour is regarded as a commodity, as an insurance, as a source of labour and as a social burden'.

In the earlier times children were part of the artisanal and agricultural labour force who worked mostly within their families. The work load allowed them time to play and to interact with other children.

The British Rule and the factory system that came closely on its heels changed the situation. Children moved far away from their native villages and worked in hazardous industries in urban areas. Exploitation of the children really started with the change in the nature of work done by the working children who came from poor families belonging to lower levels in the social hierarchy.

While pauperisation of the people in the lower social strata brought on by British Rule became the main cause for child labour, growing urbanisation and industrialization provided the scope for its use.

In the new reckoning child labour assumed the proportion of 'a problem'. The seriousness of the problem rose day by day. Today child labourers are not employed in large and medium industrial units. Thousands of economically active children are found working in small workshops, cottage industries, handicraft units and in almost all commercial manufacturing units. Most of the children are engaged in the making of glass bangles, carpets, matches, locks, readymade garments, biris and fire work. A large number of children are working in slaughter houses and also as domestic hands.

An ILO study noted, 'Small undernourished children are working for long hours, seven days a week, for a pittance. They toil in over-crowded, poorly lighted, badly ventilated premises.' The study revealed that many of the children are girls.

Though child labour is a global problem, it has assumed serious proportions in developing countries like India, Pakistan and Bangladesh. The ILO Bureau of Statistics working in Ghana, India, Pakistan, Senegal and Turkey estimated that out of 250 million working children in the age group of 1 to 14 in the developing world, 61% belong Asia. The largest number of these children are in India forming about 25% of the total.

In percentage terms working children constitute just 80% of the total labour force in India. But their contribution to GNP is much larger than their share in the labour force. A large number of these children work in export-based industries like carpet making, brass works, diamonds etc. The low wage paid to the child workers gives their employers a comparative advantage in the international market and exports they effect. This induces the employers to rely increasingly on child labour.

An Asian Labour Monitor report states that child labour in India contributes more than one fifth of the GNP. Since most child labourers get a paltry reward it would indicate that bulk of their contribution is appropriates by the employers and parents. This shows the extent of exploitation and neglect of child workers.

All the facts noted above point to the significant role of child labour in the Indian Economy notwithstanding the fact that it is a social evil.

The asset value of child labour to society would reckon them as mere instruments of income. But the loss it entails to society and the children themselves in terms of lost childhood privileges and pleasures as also lost opportunities of human resource development are immeasurable.

The evil system needs to be abolished. There is not much difference of opinion on this count. But the intricate nature of its wide prevalance, deep entrenchment in the social fabric of the country makes the problem rather difficult to solve.

It is generally believed that poverty, illiteracy, unemployment, low wages to adult labourers, social customs and population explosion are the major factors that have contributed to the growth of the child labour problem.

Since most of the causes are associated with poverty and the poor sections, there is strong feeling that unless poverty is eradicated child labour will persist. But decades of planned development and implementation of poverty alleviation programmes have not made any dent on the problem of poverty as even after 50 years of independence more than one-third of the population lives below the poverty line. If we accept the linkage of child labour with poverty the abolition of the problem in near future does not appear possible. It is, therefore, that the UNICEF Report on World's children 1997, emphasises the need to take urgent steps to tack be child labour problem and not wait till poverty is eradicated.

But poverty cannot be ignored in any plan to eliminate child labour. Child labourers come from ST, SC and lower classes, Muslims who are known to be very poor. The social customs with some of these sections of people also induces them to send their children to work places rather than to schools. In contrast, all children of upper classes invariably begin their life in schools. The UNICEF study says that dominant group do not send their children to do hazardous jobs even at their own work places but they donot mind children of ethnic, racial and economic minorities doing such work.

The UNICEF Report further states, 'In India, the view has been that some people are born to rule and the work with their minds while others, the vast majority, are born to work with their bodies.'

Even rich families in some of the lower classes who are above the poverty line send their children to work places to learn skills like scooter/motor repair, cycles repair, haircutting, tractor, engine repair, carpet weaving, brass work, tailoring, carpentry, masonary work etc., rather than send them to school.

Scholars like C.P. Chandrasekhar do not think that child labour is an upshot of poverty. He cites the case of rich states like Andhra Pradesh, Rajasthan, Tamilnadu, Karnataka and Maharastra where the incidence of child labour is higher than in poorer states like U.P., Bihar and Orissa. But while assessing the extent of child labour in a state we should also take into account the extent of urbanisation and industrialisation along with poverty. The rich states named in his study reflect these characteristics in greater measure than their poor states. Most of the hazardous occupations where children are employed arise mainly due to urbanisation and industrialisation.

PART II

The programme of national building started after independence focussed mainly on socio-economic development. Broad objectives of high growth rate, employment generation, reduction of economic indequalities and poverty alleviation were set for the five year plans that were launched in succession. The development strategy that was adopted for the purpose assigned the central place to the public sector; a regulated private sector was expected to work in tandem. As a sequel, the plans sought to bring about a social order that would ensure for every one a rightful place in society; including the children, of course.

In the early years of planning no direct measure to tackle the problem of child labour was contemplated. Over the years, in the cauldron of public debate and discussion only that segment of child labour crystalised as a problem which involved engagement of children in hazardous work. It was as late as in 1986 that for the first time a law was enacted which prohibited engagement of children in certain industries classified as hazardous. But employment of children in general was not banned.

It would thus appear that the government in India banked on the Western experience with child labour which disappeared gradually in course of economic advancement without any specific effort being directed towards its abolition. It still remains to be seen whether the historical factors that contributed to economic advancement of the west and consequent termination of child labour would be available to us and the other underdeveloped countries.

Our disillusionment with state-led development after four decades of its working set us rethinking about its relevance. Most other underdeveloped countries who followed the same course had similar experience. So all these countries, including India, tended to accept the argument of the International Monetary Fund, the World Bank and the World Trade Organisation in favour of Liberalisation, Privatisation and Globalisation, known in shorty as LPG.

India formally initiated a package of economic reforms in 1991 which were aimed at liberalisation of controls, privatisation of public enterprises and freer trade with other countries on a multilateral basis. These together are expected to pave the way for globalisation. In the economic sense globalisation means 'the transmultinationalisation of production and capital and extension of market, reach across the world.'

Such economists as Bhagwati and Srinivasan who support

the market-mediated approach argue that structural reforms in India became necessary because we failed to generate adequate rates of growth of national income and per capital income with the help of the state-led growth model.

Here, we should bear in mind that in terms of their relevance to the problem of child labour both the newly accepted market-mediated approach and the now discarded state mediated approach are based on the same logic-growth will set in motion forces that will help tackle many problems including the child labour problem. While the earlier strategy, in recognition of its shortcomings, adds supplemental steps like direct measures for poverty alleviation and improvement of health and educated by the state, the new approach considers growth as the panacea to all ills.

Now that we are through the reforms for a decade or so it remains to be seen how far have these reforms succeeded in promoting high rates of growth and in reducing poverty.

In the early years of planning the real GDP growth rate average a mere 3.5 per cent. Most of it was accounted for by a sharply rising population so that whatever remained in balance helped per capita income to rise only nominally. However, its faring during the decade 1981-90 was much better as it grew at the rate of 5.5 per cent according to National Accounts Statistics. During the reform years *i.e.*, 1991-2000, GDP grew at around 6 per cent. These rates are nowhere near the fabulous growth rate of above 12 per cent that reform promised.

What is more, the less-than-expected growth rate did not affect all section favourably. This becomes evident when we see the number below the poverty line at the end of nearly a decade of reforms. During the pre-reform years poverty eradication programmes had put some people, though not many, across the poverty line. The poverty situation has become worse after the reforms. According to estimates by S.P. Gupta in 1998 the number of people below the poverty line was 43.01 per cent which in terms of numbers works out to 430 million. This estimate is higher than all other estimates. But even going by other estimates which put it at about 36-37 per cent, the size of population below the poverty line still would appear rather large.

A positive, though low rate of rise in per capita income and rising rate of the people below the poverty line would clearly indicate that economic inequalities are widening. This is borne out by an estimate made by Raghavendra Jha in terms of real income consumption. Regular employment with adequate real wages is the best entitlement to fight poverty and food insecurity. It also offers the possibility of extending amenities like education to children. Several studies conducted to assess the impact of reforms on labour show that these have led to informalisation of the labour market, casualisation of labour and feminisation of unsilled work force. These have negative effects on the working class.

In India nearly 90 per cent of employment is in the informal sector such as agriculture, self employment, casual labour etc. Economic Survey, 2000, shows that during the last decade (1991-1999) growth rate of employment in public sector is zero while that in the private sector is very neligible. So employment opportunities are to be created in the unorganised, informal sector. Casualisation of labour is a reform phenomenon as it fits into marketisation brought on by the reform process. The brunt of casualisation and feminisation of urban labour falls on the unskilled sections of labour whose wages are low and uncertain. This has become the major cause of immiserisation of labour during globalisation.

A study of the impact of globalisation on poverty must refer to its effects on human development particularly in terms of public health and educational facilities available to the poor. As part of fiscal discipline government kept curtailing expenditure on public health and primary education and education at other levels as can be seen from Economic Survey of Government of India for different years of the reform period. Thus, the negative effect of curtailment of expenditure by Government on public health and education, on poverty eradication is very much evident. The public sector banks with a network of branches in remote rural areas served a useful purpose of actuating small savings and promoting enterprises of small farmers, artisans, traders and small entrepreneurs by furnishing loans on easy terms. They were performing a socially useful and economically rewarding task. In the name of financial sector reforms their activities are restricted and non-profit branches are closed. This has affected the disadvantaged sections.

Abolition of food, fertiliser and other subsidies, shrinkage of public distribution system that supplied essential goods to the poor at subsidised prices, withdrawal of assistance to export-based industries as also protection to import-substitution industries all tend to produce adverse effects on the poor sections of the people.

The main burden of economic reforms is borne by the poor of this country but these have not yielded the promised results in the form of high rate of growth. It is unlikely to come about in the near future, if going by all available indications noted here.

However, an important fact has emerged. It is that a rising growth rate of 6 per cent per annum during reforms period which is higher than that in the earlier period has not helped even a small number of people to get across the poverty line. On the other hand, the percentage and number of people below the poverty line is found to be rising. This clearly means that the benefits of growth do not trickle down to the poor to improve their plight and help them tide over their difficulties. Thus globalisation appears to be based on a flawed logic; and, it is, therefore, not likely to throw up a solution to the main economic problems like low growth, unemployment and poverty which the country faces. It is futile to look for an answer to child labour problem in the economic reforms and the globalisation process. Though formally launched in 1991, reforms are implemented in stages. It would thus appear premature to judge them by their performance. But we cannot overlook the fact that it hardly made any positive contribution. Most of its economic effects are negative. The growth rate registered is no better than the preceding period; there is a real setback in case of poverty alleviation, employment generation and in other areas meant to help the poor. This must have prompted its proponents to implant a welfare apparatus to protect the interest of the weak and the vulnerable against the ravages of free market. This amount to admission of inadequacy of the LPG strategy to tackle poverty and poverty-related problems like child labour.

To-day globalisation has spread to many countries in the world. But most third world countries who came under its wings are disillusioned. Millions of children in these countries are forced to do hard work in factories, mills, brick kilns and in other hazardous occupations or even scavenge for bits of food for survival. Thus, children in developed countries have all amenities and much more. Many of them as a result have fallen prey to social evils like drugs, alcohol and violence.

Jeremy Seabrook has rightly remarked, "There has always been insufficiency but during the intense globalisation the difference between privileged and non-privileged classes became larger"

With a Keen eye for the essential point Seabrook observes, 'the have-it-all kids, then become consumers of goods that many have been made by kids their age in the third world nations. It is a symbiotic relation between privileged and poverty.

It is futile to look for a solution to our child labour problem in the replication of experience of the developed countries.

As Jeremy Seabrook puts it, 'the colonial inheritance of Europe, the destruction of indigenous cultures in Australia and U.S., provided access to raw materials, land, wealth,.......... How can poor grow rich, who whill they throw out, who can they colonise to grow rich.' Have they to look for colonies in Jhompris and ghettos and resources in garbage heaps?

India must, therefore, address directly to the reality of child labour situation which has become grim under globalisation.

2

Child Labour : Causes, Consequences & Cure

—Smt. Babilata Saroff

Every parent and the society wants its children to grow into good and responsible citizens. This is possible when the children are given nutritious food, proper education, good shelter, better environment, affection and direction as well as proper guidance. Lack of these facilities puts the life of the youngsters in jeopardy. Child labour is an example of this, which is a form of exploitation due to lack of protection; both from the family and the society.

WHO IS A CHILD LABOUR?

The population below the age of 15 years are treated as children. A child labour is a working child who is employed in a gainful occupation and in the process of work may be exposed to injurious work and also may be deprived of developmental opportunities. According to the International Bureau of Statistics Report of 1980, nearly 95% of the world's children in the age group ten to fifteen years, help their family at different times as unpaid workers. These unpaid child family workers should not be considered as child labour. Because a family is an economic unit where all the members are responsible for maintaining the family and in the process contributes towards the upkeep of the whole family; a child may be required to work in the house. On the other hand the meaning of child labour will be narrow if we don't consider the cases of children either self-employed or employed in the

*Smt. Saroff, Lecturer in Econ., D.A.V. College, Titilagarh, Orissa.

household/family occupations either as full time or part time workers. (Opportunity cost should be calculated). In India most of the girls are not allowed to go outside the native place and work as unpaid family workers being deprived of education and other requirements of growth and development. Hence, a broader definition of child labour should include that segment of child population which participate in paid and unpaid work.

The Encyclopaedia of Social Sciences (1959) defines child labour as "When the business of wage earnings or of participation in self or family support conflicts directly or indirectly with the business of growth and education the result is child labour.

MAGNITUDE OF CHILD LABOUR

Child labour is a global phenomenon. ILO in 1996 estimated that 250 million child labourers economically active all over the world—at least 120 million of them were on full time basis while the others were combining their work with schooling. 50 to 60 million are engaged in hazardous occupations. Regionally it is highest in Africa (41%) followed by Asia (22%) and Latin America (13%). In absolute terms of 61% of the world's child workers are in Asia excluding Japan. Table 2.1 shows an estimate of economically active children in some of the neighbouring countries of India in 1995 (as a percentage of total children 10 to 14 years).

Table 2.1

Country	*Economically active children*
Bangladesh	30.1
China	11.6
India	14.4
Pakistan	17.4
Indonesia	9.6
Japan	0.0
Nepal	45.2
Thailand	16.1

Source : ILO.

According to 1991 census child workers in India are 11.28 million whereas it was 13.5 million in 1981 and 10.7 million in 1971. The 1991 census also shows a continuous decline in the proportion of child labour to child population (12.7% in 1961, 7.1% in 1971, 6.1% in 1981 and 5.9% in 1991). The National Institute on Occupational Health estimated (based on census data) that child participation in hazardous industries has increased more than 200% between 1961 to 1981.

According to the Ministry of Labour Annual Report, 1996-97 in India Andhra Pradesh ranks 1st *i.e.* 11.2% followed by Karnataka (8.7%). Kerala is at the bottom of the list. Orissa occupies 3rd position with 8.31 lakhs child workers in 1994. Orissa accounts for 9.13% of the country's female and 5.36% of the male child workers. 87% of them are from South-West Orissa. Bidi making, brick making, rice mills, stone crushing, black smith, etc. absorb an overwhelming 66% of total child labour under hazardous occupations. Sambalpur District has 1248 male and 3563 female child workers under hazardous occupations. The NCLP in 1995 has identified 3878 child labourers (2441 male and 1347 female) in Berhampur city, the cultural and commercial centre of Southern Orissa.

District-wise distribution shows that the tribal dominated and backward Nawarangpur is at the top of the list (15.17%) followed by Mayurbhanj (10.11%), Kalahandi (6.83%) and Koraput (6.3%). It is very low for the advanced districts like Jagatsinghpur (0.19%) and Sundergarh (0.40%).

The sector-wise distribution of child labour shows a high concentration in the unorganised sector and mostly in agricultural activities in rural areas.

WHY CHILD LABOUR EXISTS

In an International Seminar on the Health of Minors, Dr. B.L. Bataur told that one child in every four children is working out of necessity. It is true irrespective of the area to which he/she belongs—whether it is developed or underdeveloped, village or semi-urban or urban area. Orissa Labour Directorate observes that 74% of total child labourers are forced to work due to abject poverty. Children work as paid and unpaid workers due to economic, social, psychological and environmental factors (there may be an overlapping of these factors).

Economic Factors

Very often children work due to the economic benefits which they bestow upon their parents or family members. Economic benefits are the benefits which the parents and/or the family members receive or expect to receive from their children in the from of regular or irregular assistance in the shape of money, food and housing, support in old age, etc. Some think their children's contribution to family income exceeds that which is spent on them.

The question of economic benefit from children arises due to poverty, burden of unproductive consumers, indebtedness, runaway population growth resulting in large family size, migration, disturbances in the traditional occupation, status maintenance in the materialistic society etc.

The so called literate, advanced, elite and modern citizens prefer child workers for the domestic sectors, construction projects, etc. because it is easy to exploit them and derive surplus value. As they are poor and children having a weak bargaining power, we take the advantage by deriving the surplus value in terms of wages paid, work done and working hours.

Social Factors

The orphans without well-wishers are compelled to work to maintain their own lives. Among the low income groups children of diseased, gambler or drug-addicted parents go for work to maintain themselves and their families.

Sometimes neglated children with step-fathers (common in western countries but countable in our society) or step-mothers are deprived of love, affection, maintenance etc. and some of them work as child labourers.

Being a victim of the gender bias, the girl children are sent to work in poor and illiterate families. Sometimes, this is done to give comfort to the male children.

Psychological Factors

Emotion, frustration and illusion among children sometimes give rise to child labour. Frustration with a feeling of deprivation of objectives and the tendency to maintain status in the materialistic society gives rise to child labour. Robert K. Morten as American sociologist in his book "Social Structure And Anomie" pointed out that economic frustration sometimes results into drug-trafficing among boys and prostitution among girls. Alber Cohen's Delinquent Sub-Culture Theory also points out that delinquent children develop their own means and goals which are against the main values.

The influences of television programmes and cinema sometimes fall on children. Ex. A child wandering round the streets and working as a labourer becomes a great businessman, politician or film actor leaves an image on them. Out of emotion and illusion they leave their houses. Sometimes the unwanted friend circle and T.V. addiction and neglect in studies hurt the parents or elders and when they punish or bitterly scold them they leave home and finally work as labourers.

The thella-walas, ice-cream sellers and hotel boys create an illusion among some children that they would be eating lot of ice-creams, sweets, samosas, etc. and work there. Being immatures, they cannot see the things happening behind the screen "how the hotel boys eat the left outs", "how the masters treat them", etc. Some children prefer to work in domestic sectors with an illusion of getting jobs in future in the offices and companies.

Environmental Factors

The effects of urbanisation and industrialisation has not changed the attitude, class system and casteism among the people after 53 years of independence also the powerful, privileged and elite classes are exploiting the innocent, ignorant and illiterate masses. We sit in conferences, tables and seminars to discuss about their well being but seldom put into practice rather encourage them.

When a child finds many like him are working and earning in his surrounding, he is also encouraged to work.

EVIL CONSEQUENCES OF CHILD LABOUR

Child labour is economically unsound, psychologically disastrous, physically dangerous and ethically a matter of great concern. The phenomenon of child labour is deep rooted in socio-economic stratification, restricted job opportunities and prevailing poverty situation in rural India. It is a social malady and one of the greatest social malaise which vibrates towards the under development of the economy without supporting qualitative population growth. The parents of the deprived group not only send their children to work but also deprive them of numerous opportunities. The parents of the deprived group not only send their children to work but also deprive them of numerous opportunities required for a healthy social living. These children reveal several characters like frustration, aggression, delinquency, inferiority complex, alienation, lack of proper motivation and identification with the school community. They are responsible for the highest educational wastage in India and also national talent. All the works they do are not harmful but their participation in work force at a tender age tells upon their physical development and deprives them of educational opportunities.

Most of our child workers are under-paid and succeptible to coercion, towards long working hours and various other harassments.

This phenomenon is reflected in the higher incidence of drop outs in rural India and higher fertility among the low income earning couples.

Economic freedom at an early age, particularly among boys encourage them to develop bad habits like gambling, drinking of country-liquor, smoking, frequent visit to cinema and other cheap sources of entertainment. The attraction towards an urban life-style results in extravagance expenditure. The wage, rather than going to the family's income pool is used by himself. Sometimes these extravagant expenditures encourage delinquent activities like pick-pocket, stealing, drug-trafficing, etc.

Problems of child labourer vary from urban to rural setting and occupation to occupation. The problems of migrant child workers are more and complex which range from practical and financial nature to problems of socialisation, family disorganisation, health recreation, education, etc.

In the domestic sector activities range from cleaning and cooking to child care, pet-care, gardening, marketing, etc. When a single pie is lost in the house he/she is the first person to be shocked. But in the agrarian society they go beyond these activities to the maintenance of livestock, protecting crops from birds and animals, weeding, etc.

The self-employed children very often face the wrath of the police, municipal employees, adults employed in the same occupation, drunkards and antisocial elements.

The most dangerous, demanding and destructive of self-worth is the job of scrap-collectors or rag-pickers. They scrounge dustbins and garbage dumps in search of paper, rags and scraps of tin, iron, glass and even food that others have thrown away. Sometimes they are seen fighting with stray dogs for a piece of mildeed bread.

In construction works and projects they carry bricks, bolders, rods, cement bags, etc. They also water constructed houses either standing on broken walls or old ladders.

In bidi-industries children are exposed to tobacco fuels which leads to tuberculosis and asthma, continuous cold etc. Irrespective of the nature of work they do almost all of them suffer from frequent cold, cough, fever, body and joint pains, cuts/wounds etc.

In carpet industries children suffer from tuberculosis and asthma, general weakness, body and joint pains. In match and fire work industries they deal with dangerous and poisonous chemicals like potassium chlorate, phosphorous and zinc oxide. Occasional explosions prove fatal to them. In stone-quarries, lock, metal and brassware industries they inhale silicon and metal dust and face respiratory problems. In fish pealing centres they have to work continuously after the arrival of fish till the work completes.

Lack of trade-education and formal training as well as early employment affect their physical health, reduces earning capacity in the long run, sometimes mental health and life span. Though child labour supplements the family income to some extent, it reduces the income generation by lowering the wage rate and escalating adult unemployment and under employment.

EXISTING LEGISLATIVE MEASURES

In ancient times children were used to be sold as slaves for doing low and dishonourable work. Kautilya prescribed prohibition of sale of children below 8 years of age (Kautilya : Arthashastra). The ancient Indian law giver Manu has also mentioned the same in Manusmhita. To prevent and protect children from child labour, the first law was enacted in India in 1881 and since then several protective measures were enforced through new laws from time to time. Article 15(3), Article 24, Article 39(e), Article 39(f) and Article 45 of the Constitution of India—all state for the healthy development of children and free and compulsory education for all children until they complete the age of 14 years. Besides the constitutional provisions employment of children is also regulated by the Factories Act 1948, Mines Act 1952, Motor Transport Act, Plantation Labour Act 1951, Merchant Shipping Act 1958, Apprenticeship Act, Bidi & Cigarettes Act 1956 and Shops & Commercial Establishments Act 1952.

The Child Labour (Prohibition and Regulation) Act 1986 is a comprehensive law which prohibits employment of children in hazardous occupations and processes. It also regulates the working hours and bans night work. Punishment with an imprisonment for a period not less than three months for employers is also mentioned there. Any person, police officer or inspector can file a case against any employers for this offence. National Advisory Body by the Labour Department can suggest inclusion of other occupations as hazardous, as if they find.

Inspite of improval legislations like Child Labour Act 1986 and National Policy on Labour and other action programmes for the welfare of children the incidence of child labour has not come down significantly.

As per the 1993-94 report of the State Education Department of drop out rate in 1 to 5 classes is 47% and 1 to 8 is 62%. To increase enrolment, check drop outs and unversalising primary education the Government has introduced the Mid Day Meal programme from 15th Aug. 1995 and also other incentives. In Tamil Nadu, it is more successful but in Orissa, where poverty is widespread, the struggle for existence supersedes people's attitude towards education.

National Child Labour Project has also undertaken major steps like establishment of special schools to provide non-formal education, vocational training, supplementary nutrition, free books, stationaries, uniforms, mid-day meal and Rs. 100 per month to withdraw children from employment. By 1997, 76 child labour projects under the NCLP schemes have been sanctioned for covering 1.5 lakh children.

CHILD LABOUR AND THE INTERNATIONAL AGENCIES

The UNO and the ILO have also expressed serious concern and made provisions for child right and child labour elimination. Stockholm Conference in 1996 and Oslo Conference in 1997 on child right and child labour reaffirmed this as a global issue. The moralists of the west clamour for abandon or at least strict and uniform code of conduct across countries for employment of child labour. The WTO exerts pressure to maintain uniform labour standards for the protection of child labourers.

Need of the Hour

Planning and developing an appropriate strategy for elimination of child labour needs a thorough understanding of different dimensions of the problem and issues relating to the rehabilitation of child labour.

As the problem of child labour is interwoven with the basic survival issues of their families, its elimination cannot be thought of without considering a comprehensive welfare measures for their families as a whole. Long term measures like creation of conditions by providing a proper climate and social security, creation of employment opportunities available to their parents, small family norm, etc. and a package of short term measures like regulation of hours of work, weekly holidays, health recreation, safety, etc. can help tackling or at least minimising the problems of child labour.

The measures should be integrated in various national development programmes as well as action programmes implemented by the voluntary organisations. Besides, the parents of the victims, the employers and all sections of the community must be made aware of the evil consequences of child labour. Thus awareness generation through street plays, media, pamplets, rallies, etc. are necessary. The school and college students, social activists, NGOs and the media should take this responsibility as a challenge.

REFERENCES

Book

1. Becerra, Rosina M. and Xiovanmon Jeanne M., Defining Child Abuse.

Articles

1. Dek, Usha, How Protected Indian Children are?
2. Economic and Political Weekly, Dec. 4. 1999. Editorial.
3. Goyal, R.S., Problems of Child Labour in India.
4. Kanungo, Jyotirmayee, Young Girls Helping Us in our Household Work.
5. Kar, Rabi Narayan, Child Labour in India.
6. Kumar, Dr. A. and Tripathy. S.K., Child Labour in Orissa Strategies For Their Rehabilitation.
7. Kautilya, Arthashastra.

8. Mangia, Parveen, Generating Awareness on Undesirable Aspects of Child Labour.

9. Patel, S., Concepts and Measures of Child Labour.

10. Pattanik, Raghunath, Exploitation of Child Labour Law and Some Random Facts.

11. Ray, Dr. Dilip, Child Labour A Harsh Reality.

3

Socio-Economic Problem of Street Children : A Recipe

—*B.N. Dalai**

—*Dr. R.N. Misra***

THE PROBLEM

Street children create a major Social Problem in India from various view points. It is a despicable problem not only in the developing countries but also in some of the industrialized and urbanized countries of the world. Rapid emergence of the street children in developing cities of any country is a natural phenomenon all over the world as the poorest of the poor masses of the rural areas migrate to their accessible cities with a positive and comprehensive hope of getting regular employment and thereby ensuring themselves somewhat a normal life. Poor and helpless people settle in the slums, pavements and also in some cases in the backyards of some well-to-do city residents, and gradually contribute to aggravate the problem.

At the initial stage the poor immigrants find it very difficult to adjust and earn their daily bread in the new environment and ecological setting. By the way, they become individualistic in nature because of a number of interrelated factors like large family size coupled with poverty and lack of easy and immediate means to earn for the whole family. In such a situation the household head and other adults take up socially

*Deptt. of Commerce, B.J.B. College, Bhubaneswar.

**Deptt. of Commerce, Science College, Hinjilicut (Gm).

low occupations like rickshaw pulling, vending, doing petty business, working as unskilled or semi-skilled construction workers and ask their children to take up some odd jobs, like rag-picking, begging, shoeshining, cleaning train coaches and passenger buses, vending tea, egg, snacks etc. at railway platforms and bus stations, working as domestic aids and maid servants, selling fruits, doing sundry works in hotels and garages etc. and earn daily wages for self as well as for other members of their respective houses.

Generally fathers are often cruel towards their children, but mothers are relatively sympathetic. Most of the fathers are harsh because they resort to regular alcoholic drinks and spend a significant portion of their income on it. As a result, in many cases, they compel their grown up children to earn a fixed income daily. At times, when a child fails to earn the target amount fixed by his father, or when he throws himself into the playground instead of working, he is scolded, beaten up and even his meal is either reduced or denied for the day. It creates a desperate and bitter experience in the child and he prefer to away from home and to lead his life independently on the streets. He does any work he likes, eats anything he gets, and sleeps anywhere he finds suitable place, it may be railway platform, incomplete or abandoned buildings, pavements, markets, bus station or even under open sky. He forgets his family, neglects his personal hygienic care and constantly struggles for his survival.

Because of the gender discrimination, conservative Indian culture and societal norms of division of labour, the girls cannot take up any outside job like that of boys. Though a girl child is asked to work on the street with her elders for collecting rags or vending fruits or doing any such other activities, when she becomes a major, her parents try to make arrangements to engage her in less hazardous and more secured and gender specific jobs; most preferable being sundry domestic services. In this type of work, she cleans utensils, clothes, house floor, and also in some cases tends children of the employing households. She receives a meager monthly remuneration in addition to some annual incentives like new or old clothings, occasional food stuff that may be fresh or stale or leftover of previous night. At times she may receive a little festive-cash incentives.

Whatever food-incentives she gets, most often she brings the same to her home as instructed by her mother. But even though she collects various food items from different employer-households, her collection is shared either among the members of the whole family or only among the children under the supervision of her mother. Unfortunately, if she has brothers, she gets the minimum share because of the age-old traditional discriminatory practice of preference of sons over daughters in patriarchal Indian societies. Hence, she is under-nourished and her earnings are mostly shared by the whole family.

Thus, the situation of the slum children in general and the street children in particular is more vulnerable compared to their counterparts living in organized rural and urban housing settlements. Most of them lack education, immunization, sanitation, suffer from destitution and lead a life of uncertainty with insecurity

SUGGESTIVE MEASURES

The root cause of any social problem lies on the sustained persistence of an imbalance between population and available resources for utilization. In a populous country like India, human population is growing very fast due to illiteracy, low level of awareness among the rural people and flexible implementation of family planning legislations. It exerts much pressure on the local resources, and when the resources become scarce, people face various problems and migrate to resource-rich areas in order to earn their bread. Developing urban centres are such resources—rich areas which attract a number of rural wage-earning people. But when the urban centres receive more of such people than required, the available resources are over exploited and in such situations most of the children of these people come on to the streets to work and earn their own bread. As a result, in order to have complete eradication of appearance of these children on streets of urban centres, on priority basis, our national family planning measures should be implemented with utmost sincerity instead of being suggestive to have only one or two children per couple. This would, on the other hand minimize over-migration of rural people to different developing urban centres and hence proper balance between population and resources for utilizaton could be maintained. The other related suggestive measures for immediate adoption and implementation for eradication of street children would be as follows :

(a) That the municipal/corporate bodies must develop their own strategic measures to restrict over-immigration of rural wage-earners whose children most often come on to the streets for work. These corporate bodies must be very cautious to register each immigrant and not to accommodate more immigrants than required. It should endeavour to rehabilitate them properly.

(b) Those who are accommodated within the municipal area and are provided with Urban Basic Service (UBS) facilities, must be imparted awareness to strictly follow the family planning measures of the Government. In no case a family residing within the municipality be permitted to procreate more children than approved. Those, who fail to follow it, should be withdrawn from availing accommodation and land holding facility within the municipal boundary. If, for the time being these suggestive recommendations are not feasible for implementation, then the following measures may be adopted for the development and welfare of the street children.

(c) That a scientific survey be made on priority basis to identify Street-Child-households. In each slum, these children must be covered under universalization of formal education and it should be looked that they are not asked nor imposed by their parents to work as earners either on streets or at any other places. If it

happens so, then their parents must be restricted from availing ration-card facility or be withdrawn from poverty alleviation programmes, if they are covered under any such programmes.

(d) Each and every child of the slum must be provided with free education apart from free boarding facility, at least upto matriculation and there should be job guarantee for the matriculates. For the non-matriculates, need-based vocational training be provided according to their own choices and demand of the market. Provision should also be made for rehabilitation of successful trainees so that more and more street children as well as their parents would be interested and come foreword to avail of the opportunities. By this way, two-fold objectives of the nation viz., improvement of literacy and reduction of unemployment among the Indian population would be achieved.

(e) The poorest of the poor of *'At-Risk'* slum dwellers and those who live on footpaths, backyards of urban residents, under open sky, railway platforms, market complex premises, office premises etc. should be identified on priority basis and be covered under special poverty alleviation programmes in order to improve their economic condition. These children should be given more attention and be covered under the above job-guaranteed educational and vocational training programmes.

(f) Medical service should be provided at the door step of each and every slum dweller periodically, *i.e.,* at least once in a week through public mobile-health-check-up-camps/vans. Emphas is must be given to check up each child and nursing mothers without fail.

(g) Since the nature and working pattern of the street children varies from one to another, Government must work out some specific legislations for the welfare of each category of these children. For example, the working nature and pattern of a domestic servant is not same as that of a hotel boy or a garage worker. Hence, there must be specific legislations indicating their nature of work, hours of work, etc. Accordingly minimum wage rates be also fixed up and specified in order to protect them from exploitation.

(h) The rag-pickers work hard throughout the day, but they are exploited at various levels; one level being at the local godown keepers where they sell their collections. Since there is no uniform rate-charts for different rag-items, the innocent rag-pickers fall prey to various godown keepers. So, Government must take proper initiatives to fix-up uniform rates for different scraps and the godown keepers must be instructed to display the rate-charts for public and work accordingly.

(i) Relating to the above suggestions, there should be a special consumer court to which the children can have an easy access and approach to lodge complaints.

(j) As an alternative to the above suggestion *(i)*, it would be better if municipal corporate bodies fix up some collection centres, and collect rags from rag-pickers from such centres through mobile collection vans. If it is done so, in one hand these corporate bodies would raise their own revenue and on the other hand the rag-pickers would get proper value of their collections and hence also get relieved from being exploited by the local godown keepers.

(k) As the street children are deprived of availing public parks, play grounds etc, for relaxation, slum-based recreational facilities play grounds be developed and game items be provided by the municipal corporate bodies.

(l) Government should take immediate steps to identify the orphans who work on streets, railway stations etc. on priority basis and must try to accommodate them in orphanges financed by union or state Government or NGOs funded by foreign agencies.

(m) Like the orphans, girl children of the street should also be identified on priority basis and specific need-based self employment programmes be formulated for them. Specifically, they should be imparted training on some vocational trades like sewing, applique work, terracotta work and other handicrafts out of which they can independently earn their livelihood. However, there must be a cooperative institution at the Government level to procure the products from these children at a reasonable price fixed by the Government. This would, in other way, help them to get suitable life partners for marriage.

(n) It is universally realised that if we educate a man, we educate a person but if we educate a woman, we educate a family. So, apart from providing vocational training, girl children should also be provided with formal or non-formal education depending upon their age and interest.

(o) Finally, a special committee be formed at the Government level to facilitate proper implementation of the welfare schemes and to protect the street children from exploitation.

REFERENCES

1. Arimpoor, Joe (1992), Street Children of Madras, Noida : National Labour Institute.
2. BMC (Bhubaneswar Municipal Corporation) (1995), Paura Samachar (Oriya), Bhubaneswar.
3. Butterflies (1994), My Name is Today, Children News, Vol. II, No. 2, April-June, New Delhi.
4. Centre for Youth and Social Development (1991), Directory of Voluntary Organisations in Orissa, Bhubaneswar.
5. CPSW (Council of Professional Social Workers) (1998), CPSW News, Vol. I, No. I, Bhubaneswar.
6. Felsman, J.K. (1985), Street Children : A Selected Bibliography, Hannover, USA (ERIC).

7. G.O.I. (Govt. of India), (1971), Special Survey Reports on Selected Towns : Bhubaneswar, Series 16, Orissa, Part. IIB.

8. G.O.I. (Govt. of India), (1997), 'Child Labour and Street Children' in DPEP Calling, New Delhi : Department of Education.

4

Child Labour in Carpet Industry

(A Study of Legal Implications)

—*Dr. S.N. Tripathy**

—*Sri Kedar Nath Bisoyee***

The problem of child labour had raised its ugly head since the dawn of industrial revolution in Europe and other countries. The problem of object poverty, backwardness, unemployment and low-level of income has resulted in vicious circle binding the children in various hazardous and non-hazardous occupation. It is estimated that about 50 million children in India are in the grip of exploitation and child labour. They are extensively engaged in agriculture, carpet industry, bidi rolling, brick-kilns, construction sectors and other.

Child labour refers to work undertake by a child, who is below 15 years of age, for wages or it refers to employment of in the socio-economic scenario like rapid urbanisation, rural-urban migration, distintegration of joint-family and community structure have given birth to vulnerable group of children known as migrant child labour. They are the most neglected, deprived, uneducated, uncared children who struggle for their survival. Child labour is economically unsound, psychologically disastrous and physically as well as mentally dangerous and harmful. It deprives of educational, training and skills to a child. Due to their vulnerability children are exploited, illustrated and employed in the undesirable channels, by unscrupulous and anti-socials in the community.

*Dept. of Economics, Post-Doctoral Fellow, Aska Science College, Aska, (Orissa).

**Project Director, National Child Labour Project, Malkangiri, Orissa.

In our country, the migrant child labourers are found ragpicking, selling lottery tickets at traffic lights, shinning shoes, hawking newspapers etc. Thus, they are neglected by and segregated from society, excluded from Government policy, deprived of education and basic services, subject to physical danger and exploited by unscrupulous adults on the street and in most cases by the Police. The emergence of the problem of migrant child labour owes its origin from frequent crop failures and recurring droughts, assetlessness and candlessness of the parents, distressed living conditions, indebtedness and bondage etc. (Tripathy, 1991).

MAGNITUDE OF THE PROBLEM

Child Labour though a universal phenoneon is certainly a social evil.

The magnitude of child labour is infact, high in the developing countries. Though the problem of child labour is manifested everywhere in the world, about 98 per cent of working children are noticed in the developing countries. According to the International Programme for the Elimination of Child Labour (IPEC) Document (1992), the number of working children in the world ranges between 100 and 200 million.

The Human Development Report (1993) of United Nations Development Programme (UNDP) reveals that child labourers are among the world's most exploited workers. Hundreds of billions of children work in fields & factories, in street corners and in garbage dumps all over the world.

In India, most of the children are employed in cottage industries, producing carpets, matches, fire crackers, cigarettes, brassware, diamonds, glass, hosiery, handloom cloth, embroiding, bangles and traditional handicrafts.

Existence of child labour in the tribal areas in Orissa are largely found in the districts of Mayurbhanj, Bolangir, Kalahandi, Koraput, Keonjhar and Phulbani.

It is found that the social customs, obligations like birth, marriages, death in the families and drinking habits play an important role in compelling the destitute families to resort to borrowing. The money lenders take the advantage of the distressing economic situation of the poverty-stricker parents and advance loans from time to time so as to compel the poor parents to go abroad seeking employment in construction projects, brick-klins etc. alongwith their children, resulting in mass reasonal migration and drop-outs. This has been manifested in the tribal dominated districts of Kalahandi, Koraput, Bolangir and Sundargarh of Orissa (Tripathy & Das 1997 Tripathy, 1997).

CHILD LABOUR IS CARPET INDUSTRY

At a rough estimate of 2 lakhs of children work in the carpet industry and they do the major part of the work. The industry could not survive without the children. A carpet is not woven, it is knotted, and each individual knit has to be made by hand. Eighty per cent of knotting work is done by children under the age of 16. Weaving carpets is convenient with the 'humble fingers' of children. It is also exclusively used in the fireworks industry in Sivakasi where three years olds work with inflammable explosived. It goes without saying that these children, deprived of education are bonded children in the sense of the term. They work long hours without protests, are easily coerced and would also do a lot of unpaid work for the employer.

The huge profit earned by the owner provides an bye-law raising facts. A square yard of carpet which a boy may weave in a day can sell for an amount between Rs. 200 to 700 in the export market. For that the boy who actually made it is paid the amount of Rs. 20 to 30. And from it the loom owner will deduct the expense of food, medicine and clothes.

It is obvious from the analysis that the whole system is organised to exploit the children to the maximum. Most of the children employed in areas around Varanasi, in Khamaria, Aurali, Gopigunj and in the district of Mirzapur and brought to the weaving centre through recruiting agents from the tribal areas of Bihar like Sitamar and Palaman. Their parents are usually belonging to weaker sections of the society, poverty-stricken and landless labourers. The agents alluve them to provide better payments and equip the children with skill so as to support the family. The agents provide loans to the poverty-ridden families and then take their children as bondage to the carpet weaving Industry to work at the carpet looms. The agents have adhered to this recruiting system not because of shortage of child labour but due to the fact that segregated 10-12 years children away from their family can be exploited conveniently.

A child usually requires about six months to learn to knot carpets. But the loom owner terms him a Chela or learner for anywhere upto three years and in this period he is paid nothing and only gets a two means a day. By the time a boy is about 15, he becomes a master weaver.

The system works in three tiers and is designed to circumvent the laws and more the exporters beyond the legal responsibilities. The exporters supply the loom owners with the material of wool and thread and the design with specific orders of carpets. These middlemen loom owners never perform the actual weaving. They have set-up looms in their villages in isolated huts where the child weavers work and reside. As the looms are scattered over hundreds of villages, it is not a heculean task to monitor the condition of children without a minimum of 20 children working under the same roof their rights to basic medical and financial benefits are not protected as it does not fall within the purview of the factory Act.

The exporters are concentrated in Khamaria and in the town of Bhadohi. They have very carefully removed themselves from the actual process of production so they can safely announce that they do not employ children.

In the back-drop of the aforesaid analysis, it is imperative to focus the legal enactments and provisions made from time to time to safeguard the interest of the child labour in Indian States.

LABOUR ENACTMENTS

For the benefits of children and adolescents engaged in specific occupations and industry there are as much as eleven labour enactments in our country. These are as follows :

(i) Factories Act, 1948.

(ii) Minimum Wages Act, 1948.

(iii) Doct Workers' Regulation & Employments Act, 1948.

(iv) Plantation Labour Act, 1951.

(v) Mines Act, 1952.

(vi) Merchant Shing Act, 1958.

(vii) Motor Transport Workers Act, 1961.

(viii) Apprentice Act, 1961.

(ix) Radiation Protection Rules, 1971, under the Atomic Energy Act, 1962.

(x) Bidi and Cigar Workers (Condition of Employment) Act.

(xi) Shops and Commercial Establishment Acts under various nomenclatures in states.

Thus, it is found that the constitution of India, both in the Directive principles of State Policy and as a part of the Fundamental Rights, had laid down that the State shall direct its policy towards securing that health and strength of workers, men and women, and the tender age of children are not abused, and that citizens are not forced by economic necessity to enter vocations unsuited to their age for strength, and that children, particularly, are given opportunities and facilities to develop in a healthy manner and in conditions of freedom and dignity. Childhood and youth are to be protected against exploitation, and no child below the age of 14 years shall be employed to work in any factory or mine or engaged in any other hazardous employment.

The National Policy for Children Resolution, adopted in August 1974, further developed the above ideas, and set out a Policy framework and measures aimed at providing adequate services for children. These were to form a prominent part of the nation's plan for development of human resources. Free and compulsory education for all children upto the age of 14, provision of health and nutritional programmes and services, providing alternative forms of education for children unable to take full advantage of formal school education—for whatever reasons—and measures for protecting children against neglect, cruelty and exploitation form part of the national Policy for Children. The Policy also provides, as one of its objectives, that no child under the age of 14 years shall be permitted to be engaged in hazardous occupations or be made to undertake heavy work.

The Committee on Child Labour (Gurupadaswamy Committee) which submitted its report in December, 1979, examined the problems of child labour in detail. India is one of the countries where the problems of child labour are quite openly manifest, and the widespread existence of child labour has been viewed by the Government of India with concern. The Gurupadaswamy Committee recognised that a distinction had to be made between child labour and the exploitation of child labour as, though both are a problem, they are of different orders. It had underlined that in all future action dealing with child labour this basic aspect would have to be taken note of, *i.e.*, that "labour becomes an absolute evil in the case of the child when he is required to work beyond his physical capacity, when hours of employment interfere with his education, recreation and rest, when his wages are not commensurate with the quantum of work done, and when the occupation he is engaged endangerous his health and safety" *i.e.* when he is exploited.

Government has given consideration to these aspects of the problem of child labour, *i.e.*, the need to protect child labour from exploitation or from being subjected to work in hazardous conditions which endanger such children's physical and mental development; the need to ensure safety and health at their working places, that they should be protected from excessively long working hours and from night work, and that there should be regulated work even in non-hazardous occupations, and that all child labour have to be sufficient weekly rest periods and holidays in their employments.

The recently enacted Child Labour (Prohibition and Regulation) Act, 1986, is the culmination of the process of consideration that Government has been giving to this pervasive problem figuring in the economic & social landscale in the country. Both in enacting this legislation, and thereafter in proceeding to lay down the policy and the outside of the programme of action, Government have had to keep the in mind the economic and social aspects of child labour in the country. For example, with substantial portions of Gross Domestic Product (GDP) coming from the agricultural sector, from rural industries or from artisan's workshops, or from small scale services, often children work as an essential part of a farm household, or as part of the working family assisting parents in ancillary tasks. In such working activities by children in farm and field, in artisan households or in small family-centred trade or service establishments, children most often acquire the skills which enable them to become full-fledged workers in farming households, family establishments or trades. While work of such kinds has its problems, it is more essential at the present stage of our national development to concentrate in those sectors or establishments where children are deployed on wage or quasi-wage employment, outside the family, where there is most likely to arise exploitation, in whatever form it may be.

The national anti-poverty policies, the national education policy, the National Policy on health for all and on nutrition, as also the generally stepped-up provisions in social services in national plan outlays, are all geared to tackle the problems of poverty, where too often the origins and compulsions of child labour are rooted. The general raising of large numbers of the population above the poverty line, or the provision of the entire spectrum of improved social services in the areas above mentioned will, it is hoped, lead to progressive elimination of poverty, and consequently of the phenomena of children being put out for wage employment or quasi-wage employment at unsuitable ages. The measures to promote employment-oriented development both in rural and in urban areas, and the all-round development and extention of adequate facilities for both formal and non-formal education, vocational education and training, and in the coverage and extension of social security and family welfare measures would all go a long way to tackle the basic and root causes of child labour.

This action programme, therefore, has to be viewed against the above background. Specifically, the attempt is to deal with a situation where children work, or are compelled to work, on a regular or a continuous basis to earn a living for themselves and/or for their family, and where their conditions of work resulted in their being severely dis-advantaged and exploited, and where abuses connected with such factors impacting on wage-employed children need to be given close attention by the State for rectification, amelioration and regulation through specific legal and administrative instruments and measures.

ESTABLISHMENT OF NATIONAL AUTHORITY FOR ELIMINATION OF CHILD LABOUR

A major step towards the elimination of child labour in hazardous employments was taken by the Minister of State for Labour on 1 October, 1994 when the National Authority for the Examination of Child Labour was set up under his Chairmanship. The functions of the National Authority for Elimination of Child Labour are :

1. to lay down the policies and programme for elimination of child labour particularly in hazardous employments;
2. to monitor the progress of implementation of programmes, project and schemes for elimination of child labour.
3. to co-ordinate implementation of child labour

elimination related projects of the various sister Ministers of the Government of India.

The National Authority for Elimination of Child Labour has met three times so far since its formation on 1st October, 1994, the 1st November, 1994 and 16th January, 1995. In its third meeting held on 16th January, 1995, the NAECL adopted a blue print for action to tackle the child labour problem titled "Identification, Release & Rehabilitation of Child Labour." The circular has been forwarded to the States/UTs for adoption.

This Circular covers the range of actions required to tackle the child labour problems especially in hazardous occupations. Briefly it calls for a convergence of service and schemes of the Central and State Governments at the implementing level—the district level to effectively handle the child labour elimination effort. Broadly, this effort aims at :

(a) better enforcement of laws intended for the protection of children;

(b) Withdrawing of children from work and diverting them to special schools where they will be given primary level education, vocational training and nutrition and stipends;

(c) Covering parents of child labour through poverty alleviation and income generation schemes to reduce their need to send their children to work;

(d) Prevent fresh entry to children into occupations from which child labour has been withdrawn by intensifying activities to provide pre-school education, health and nutrition to children in the 0-6 age group through schemes like ICDS, Community Nutrition Programme.

The Ministry of Labour has also drafted a detailed scheme to eliminate child labour in hazardous occupations (ECHO) through special educational inputs, better enforcement of laws, health care, nutritional and stipendry inputs in addition to vocational training. This draft proposal is under examination.

The ECHO Project is targetted at 11 States (A.P., U.P., T.N., Bihar, Rajasthan, Gujarat, Maharashtra, West Bengal,

Orissa and Karnataka) which together account for nearly 90% of the child labour population of the country.

INTERNATIONAL IMPACT OF CHILD LABOUR

The Utilisation of Child labour in some export-oriented industries like carpet manufacturing has adversely affected India's image. There are moves in U.S.A. and other Western countries to ban the import of goods produced with the help of child labour.

INTERNATIONAL COOPERATION IN TACKLING THE PROBLEM OF CHILD LABOUR

In order to show India's commitment to tackle the problem of child labour effectively, the country has been a participant in the I.L.O's International Programme for the Elimination of Child Labour. Over 30,000 children are presently covered under IPEC.

In addition the Government of India's efforts to tackle the child labour problem has been assisted by the I.L.O's initiative called Child Labour Action Support Programme (CLASP). The UNICEF has also contributed to this country's efforts in child labour elimination.

ILO-AIDED PROJECTS

The Government proposes to launch 20 additional projects in the country under the ILO-aided International Programme on elimination of child labour. These projects will be implemented in close co-operation with the State Governments and other agencies such as voluntary Organisations, trade unions and employers Association.

It is estimated that these projects are expected to benefit directly and indirectly, 16,005 and 63,000 child labourers respectively. About 3,86,030 parents of child labourers will receive the benefits of such projects.

Aimed at progressive elimination of child labour from the project areas, these projects seek to tackle the problem of child labour through better enforcement of laws, focussing of development programmes relating to poverty alleviation and providing adult-education.

PROJECT : ELIMINATION OF CHILD LABOUR IN HAZARDOUS TO OCCUPATIONS (ECHO)

Run up to Project ECHO

1. On August 15, 1994, the Prime Minister announced the Programme of Eliminate Child Labour in Hazardous Occupations in the Elimination of Child Labour in Hazardous Occupations (ECHO).
2. A meeting was held under the Chairmanship of Minister of State for Labour with the 17 Labour Ministers/Labour Secretaries on 2nd September, 1999 to discuss the child labour problems.
3. Formation of National Authority for the Elimination of Child Labour on 26th September, 1994.
4. The issue of child labour was discussed in the Labour Ministers Conference held in July, 1993, Standing Labour Committee held on 27th October, 1994 and the Indian Labour Conference held on 3rd & 4th January, 1995.
5. The Child Labour Advisory Board was reconstituted on 2nd November, 1994.
6. The Circular on "Identification, Release and Rehabilitation of Child Labour" was adopted by NAECL on 16.01.95.
7. The Draft Proposal for ECHO is ready and is under examination. (January, 1995).
8. Planning Commission approves an initial outlay of Rs. 34.4 crores for ECHO (January, 1995).

Broad Features of ECHO in Draft Proposal

1. 1.8 million children @ Rs. 3256 per child per year; Each child will be given 3 years of special primary level education.
2. 18,000 Schools.

3. 36,000 Teachers.
4. 18,000 Vocational Training instructors.
5. 2000 enforcement officers to be trained.
6. Establishment special mechanisms for decentralised handling of child labour elimination effort.
7. Special Awareness inputs to sensitize parents in child labour prone areas, employers society.
8. Special intensification of Enforcement Authority.
9. Aim at a district level convergence of services and schemes of Government.
10. Prevent fresh entry of child into work.

Implementation of ECHO will be done in a phased manner between 1995 and 2002.

AMBITIOUS RS. 850 CRORES SCHEME

The Government of India has formulated an ambitious Rs. 850 crores scheme to eliminate child labour in the manufacturing and services sectors over a five years period. It has been proposed for a national authority which will raise funds for various rehabilitation programmes for 20 lakhs working children.

Plans for a phased elimination of child labour in hazardous and exploitative occupations have been drawn. The five-year scheme aims at eliminating child labour by the turn of the century.

The scheme is to be concentrated on seven states of Andhra Pradesh, Bihar, Karnataka, Madhya Pradesh, Maharashtra, Tamilnadu and Uttar Pradesh which account for 73 per cent of the country's child labour population.

The dimensional activities under the scheme include setting up of Centres for non-formal education with prevocational content, provision for nutritional needs and basic health cover, and multi-media projection on awareness creation among the local populace.

An elaborate enforcement machinery will be created and for this assistance would be given to the state of appoint special staff. At the field, level, assistance will also be given to non-government organisations to implement programmes.

Among the occupations deemed to be hazardous for children are bidi-making, carpet-weaving, cement manufactures and begging, cloth printing dyeing and weaving, manufacture of matches, explosives and fireworks, mica-cutting and splitting, soap manufacturing, tanning, building & construction industry, and manufacturing processes using such substances as lead, mercury, manganese and asbestos.

It has been observed that industries which violate the law know from past experience that bureaucratic apathy and lack of political will can be exploited to get away scot-free as they did when the government drew-up an ambitious plan last year to withdraw concessions to industries employing child labour. It is nobody's contention that the Government can wave a magic ward and do away with child labour over-night, but what is appalling is that there is no fresh thinking on the subject.

Countries like the USA and Germany are introducing legislation to prevent imports of goods from India & other developing countries ostensibly for using child labour with little thought for the fate of the children who may be deprived of their livelihood before other provisions are made for them. This sort of trade protectionism under the guise of concern for poor children sits ill on countries like the US which have been able to do little to prevent their economically disadvantaged children from taking to the streets and engaging them in hazardous occupations.

REFERENCES

1. Tripathy, S.N., Exploitation of Child Labour in Tribal India, Daya Publishing House, Delhi, 1991.
2. Tripathy, S.N. & Das C.R., Migrant Labour in India, Discovery Publishing House, New Delhi, 1997.

3. Tripathy, S.N., Migrant Child Labour in India, Mohit Publication, New Delhi, 1997.
4. Gupta, Subhadra Sen, Children of Darkness, Indian Express, 4th Sept, 1988.
5. *Ibid.*
6. *Ibid.*
7. Tripathy, S.N., Migrant Child Labour in India, *op. cit.*
8. *Ibid.*

5

Migrant Child Labour—A Study of India in Hazardous

*—R.L. Panigrahy**

Child Labour is defined as a person who has not completed the age of 14 years according to Child Labour (Prohibition & Regulation) Act, 1986. It is supported with Minimum Wages Act, 1948, Plantation Act, 1951, Merchant Shippling Act, 1958, Motor Transport Act, 1961.

According to International Labour Organisation (ILO) 2 million are engaged in hazardous occupations like carpet work, glass work, fire works, chemical works, industries, etc. As UN estimates in every 5 working children, 1 is from India.

CAUSES OF MIGRANT CHILD LABOUR :

1. Economic marginality
2. Unequal wealth and income distribution
3. Unbalanced economic development
4. Scarcity of employment and agriculture development in rural areas
5. Chronic and acute poverty
6. Frequent crop failure and drought
7. Assetless and landlessness of parents
8. Distributed living conditions

*Mr. Rajib Lochan Panigrahy is working as a Lecturer in Computer Science & Management in Swami Sivananda Polytechnic, Aska (Under Berhampur University).

9. Indebtedness and bondage
10. Over crowded homes
11. Parent abuses
12. Drug abuses of parents
13. Alcoholism of parents
14. Parent abandoning child
15. Run away child due to socio-economic stain on them

ENGAGEMENTS OF CHILD LABOUR

Children were employed in hazardous occupations like factories, match works, beedi works, glass works, lubricating works, chemical works, liquor shops, leather and shoe industries, prostitutions, etc. Most of the child labourers are illiterate and outside from his family, supplement his family. Every third household in India has a working child and the child labour contributes over 20% of India's Gross National Product (GNP).

WORLD SCENARIO OF CHILD LABOUR

The existence of child labour in South-East Asia and Asian countries has become a matter of international concern during the present decade. More than 80% of the working children belongs to Asia from the rural areas and unorganized primary sector of the economy.

Distribution of Child Labour in the World

Continent	*Nos. in Million*	*% of share in total*
South-East Asia	29	55.77
Rest of Asia	9.1	17.50
Africa	9.7	18.65
South America	3.1	5.96
North America	0.3	0.59
Europe	0.7	1.34
Oceania	0.1	0.19

Source : Social Welfare Feb'96, p. 28.

As per ILO estimates, in India 10,000 children are working in leather and shoe industry and in agricultural sector. In US 28% of 15 years old and 51% of 16-17 years old engaged. In Russia child labourers are increasing at a galloping speed.

CHILD LABOUR IN INDIAN SCENARIO

In India 40% of population are children. An on 1971 census 11.5% of male and 4.6% of female children were full time workers in rural India. In rural areas child labour in case of male was 57.86 and female 42.14. And in urban areas 48.30 are male and 31.70 are female children as labourers. The male child labourers constitute 58.95% and female child labourers constitute 41.05% as on 1981 census. As on 1981 census there are 13,640,872 child labourers of 4-15 years are in India.

MIGRANT CHILD LABOUR

In India migrant child labour in 1981 census was 56,083 where migrant labourers were 7,71,237. The states having its share as :

State	*in %*	*State*	*in %*
Andhra Pradesh	7.06	Tripura	0.21
Bihar	5.98	Uttar Pradesh	7.18
Gujarat	9.45	West Bengal	5.91
Haryana	2.85	Andaman & Nicober Island	0.07
Himachal Pradesh	0.99	Dadar & Nagar Haveli	0.03
Jammu & Kashmir	1.09	Mizorram	0.6
Karnataka	9.22	Pondicherri	0.20
Kerala	2.73	Orissa	4.42
Madhya Pradesh	8.17	Meghalaya	0.19
Maharashtra	9.74	Nagaland	0.16
Goa & Daman Diu	0.80	Manipur	0.11
Rajasthan	0.01	Delhi	7.26
Sikkim	3.27	Lakshadeep	0.01
Tamil Nadu	7.42	Chandigarh	0.72

Source : Tripathy S.N., Migrant Child Labour in India, p. 41-43, Discovery Publications.

MIGRANT CHILD LABOUR IN INDIA

As on 1981 census 16,064 child labourers were migrated from one state to another from rural to urban slum, out of which 64,18% migrated from rural to urban. In this figure 67.48% are male and 32.52 are female percentages of migrant child labour. But in case of Tripura, Lakshadeep, Pondicherry more female percentages are migrant child labourers.

In Tripura no rural child labour migrant and in Jammu & Kashmir, Karnataka, Kerala, Meghalaya, Sikkim, Tamil Nadu and Tripura received more urban child labour.

Migrant Child Labour from States as on 1981 with Education Standard

State	*Total Migrant Child Labour*	*Illiteracy*	*Below Matric*	*Above Matric*
1	*2*	*3*	*4*	*5*
AP	297	189	108	—
Bihar	508	392	117	—
Gujarat	954	713	241	9
Haryana	904	663	241	—
Himachal Pradesh	147	109	38	1
J & K	198	154	42	2
Karnataka	671	409	258	5
Kerala	309	189	120	—
MP	657	533	121	—
Manipur	42	31	11	—
Maharashtra	2378	1319	1319	10
Meghalaya	37	26	11	—
Nagaland	56	51	5	1
Orissa	192	148	43	—
Punjab	948	69	179	—

(Contd.).

(Contd.)

1	*2*	*3*	*4*	*5*
Rajasthan	707	576	131	—
A & N Islands	37	14	23	—
Chandigarh	403	295	103	—
WB	1267	1066	201	—
UP	506	326	183	—
Sikkim	43	31	13	—
TN	387	173	209	5
Tripura	12	8	4	—
Dadar & Nagar Haveli	7	3	4	—
Delhi	3933	3008	917	—
Goa, Daman & Diu	269	200	69	—
Lakshadeep	3	1	2	—
Mizoram	9	7	2	—
Pondicherry	79	48	31	2

CHILD LABOUR IN HAZARDOUS OCCUPATION

Child Labour at Delhi

Half a million of migrant child labourers are sexually exploited over worked, under paid, harassed domestic servants in a miserable sub-human living at Delhi. They are mostly migrant from UP, MP, Nepal and Orissa.

Child Labour in Plantation

The child labour engaged in plantation of Assam and WB are tribals from Chhotanagpur of Bihar, MP and Orissa. The labourers were permanently settled by the plantation making individuals on plantation in and around by family base. They are restricted for chemical plantation in Plantation Labour Act 1951. WB and 21,086 and Assam had 63,376 child labourers engaged in plantation as on 1981-81.

Child Labour at Calcutta

In Calcutta city of WB child labour are engaged in machinery repairs and assembly, and also batteries, cooling machines, motors, etc. All the labourers are adversely covered in ash and clay. Their physical standards are most pathetic and miserable.

Child Beggars

The destitute families produce the child beggars for their livelihood. In spite of these the migrant child labour from rural to urban or the child kidnapped are engaged as beggars by a gang man making a group in different localities in different ways and dress for begging.

Child Labour in Sivakasi (TN)

In match industries the children are engaged in match making with poisonous chemicals. The instructions are given in match items to be away from children is given in match items to be away from children. But in Sivakasi the children are engaged for match making. More than 50,000 child labour are engaged below 15 in these industries. They are working with Potassium Chlorate, Phosphorous and Zinc Oxides. They have no holidays. The child labour face explosions, casualities, back bone pains, chemical hazards.

Child Labour in Beedi Industries of Tripura & Trichur

Mostly child labour are engaged in Tiruchirapalli and Trichur of TN are girls. They are working under contract basis. It is easy to engage them in prostitution and they might be dragged for sexual intercourse. They are 2 lakhs migrant child labourers engaged in these industries.

Child Labour in Lock Industries of Aligarh

Mostly locks are build in Aligarh of. The child labourers are engaged of preparing locks with hand process, polishing colour spray, painting, filing the components of finishing, making & clipping of springs, assembling and packing of locks.

They are working rest less of 12-14 hours per day. They are suffering of fever, asthma, tuberculosis, bronchitis, etc.

Child Labourers in Carpet Weaving

As on 1978-79 handicraft census of J & K, more than 27,000 children are in handicraft industries. In an other estimation the number of working children are 30,000 in registered and unregistered carpet weaving looms. And 50 to 150 thousands of children are out of school.

In Varanasi, Bhadohi, Mirzapur belt of UP has an important role of carpet weaving and export from country 30% of its work force and children

In Rajasthan 40% workers of carpet industries are children below 15 years.

In Surat and nearby areas of Gujarat, the children are engaged in the weaving looms to arrange the unused threads used. They are mostly Marathis and Oriyas.

The child labourers of these industries face finger cut, distortion in backbone, skin problem and TB.

Child Labour in Gem Polishing

Out of 60,000 work force under survey, 13,000 are children working at Gem Polishing industries of Rajasthan. They loose eyesight.

Children Labour in Rag Picking

The most unhygienic, dangerous job in scrap collection or rag picking. The children of poverty stricken SC/ST/OBC classes or slum dweller class are engaged in such activities. They are collecting waste materials of plastic, tin, iron, bottles from garbage and dirty places of urban area. The glass or metal or iron pieces may injure their bare foots. For their bread and butter, they are working such. In rag picking the children engaged, face tetanus and skin diseases.

Child Labour in Brassware

There is an estimation of 7,000 to 10,000 children engaged in brassware industries of Moradabad. Children can be injured and lose their limbs working in moulding, polishing and fornace of 1100^0C temperature. They face eyeburn and chest diseases. And also they get loss of life. They also face bronchitis, bone disorder, muschular pain and tract infection.

Child Labour in Slate-Stone Mines of AP

In slate-stone mines of Markapur of AP, the children who are working in these industries are assets to their parents and are dropped out from school or not attended the school. The child labour are exploited or stolen. They are very cheap labourers. In this consequence, the stone-slates are exported to Singapur and Australia. The children as labourers also face the silicons.

PROTECTION OF CHILD LABOUR FROM HAZARDOUS OCCUPATIONS

Child labour is not illegal in India, but the exploitation, hazardous occupations are to be prohibited and restricted legally. Hence Govt. has taken certain legal amendments as follows.

Article 14 of Indian constitution prescribes that no child under 14 years would be made to work in any factory or a mine or engage in any other hazardous employment.

Article 39(e) directs the state to see that the tender age children are not abused and that citizens are not compelled by economic circumstances to do work that is unsuited to their age or strength.

Article 39(f) emphasizes that the need to see that childhood and young are protected against exploitation and against moral and material detriment.

Article 23 confers a Fundamental Right against certain form of exploitation. The provision of punishment for such exploitations are provided in Indian Penal Code.

Article 15(3) has special provisions for women and children.

Article 45 (DPSP) says that the state shall endeavour to provide within a period of 10 years from the commencement of the constitution free and compulsory education for all children until they complete the age of 15 years.

Child Labour (Prohibition & Protection) Act 1986 prohibits child labour in certain occupations.

Factories Act 1948 defines minimum age of employment

fixed to 14 years and 5 hours work in a day, employment during night and on hazardous occupation was prescribed.

Mines Act 1952 defines minimum of employment in mines is fixed at 15, below age children may be employed for part time or in any open excavation.

Plantation Act 1957 fixed age of employment at 12 years.

Employment of Child Labour Act 1938 was to check abuses arising out of employment in workshops which are outside the scope of factory legislation. Employment of child between 15 and 17 during night in railways and port is prohibited.

The Motor Transport Workers Act 1961 also prohibits employment of children below 14 years.

CONCLUSION

In spite of these elaborations, the child labour still exists till the BPL people and illiteracy abolishes from the country. The country should be towards full employment and the slum, poverty should be abolished, then the child labour will not find. Otherwise the child labour and all the above problems will only not exist but it will increase rapidly and will became a disease. This picture make the country miserable.

One had said "Child Labour has sweet blood and tender bones. The employers are easy to become mosquito to drag their blood, dog to drew their flesh, wolf to chew their bones and ghost to make them afraid.

REFERENCES

Social Welfare, Feb'96

1. Child Labour—Education is a key : Das U.K.
2. Child Labour—Problems and Solutions : Prof. K.L. Tiwari.
3. Child Labour—Issues and Laws : Dr. D. Vasudev Rao & Prof. B.Y. Raju.
4. Child Labour—Adults at the age of five : Mrs. Aishath Suhara.
5. Child Prostitutes and Sex Tourism : Dr. L.N. Mittal.
6. New Diary Call to adopt National Policy on Child Labour : PTI, New Delhi.

Social Welfare, Apr'97

7. Gender Perspective in Child Labour : Dr. Neeti Mohanti.
8. Restoring Childhood in Child Labour : Uma Joshi.

Social Welfare, Dec'95

9. ICDS Schemes need Revampting : Uma Joshi.
10. Report Colombo Conference—The Girl Child especially in different circumstances : B. Bhamathi.
11. Right of the child—Role of the media : Rita Puhani.

Social Welfare, Jun'95

12. Ragpicking of Bangalore : Varghose Pallipuram.

Social Welfare, Jul'90

13. Child Pledging in Beedi Industry : G. Ravindran Nair.

Social Welfare, Mar'96

14. Guarding the Girl Child : Dr. I. Satya Sundaram.

Orissa Review May-June'97

15. Child Labour in Orissa Today, p. 40 : Dr. H.K. Misra.
16. Vision September-December'98

Economics of Child and Industrial Relations 1996 Edition : Dr. T.N. Bhagoliwal

17. Child and Woman Labour, Chapter-26, p. 613.
18. Labour Policy in India, Chapter-29, p. 615.

Books

19. Migrant Child Labour in India : Dr. S.N. Tripathy, Mohit Publications, ND.
20. Bonded Labour in India : Dr. S.N. Tripathy, Discovery Publications, ND.
21. Exploiting Child Labour in Tribal India : Dr. S.N. Tripathy, Daya Publications, ND.

6

Problems of Child Labour in Hazardous Occupation

—*Dr. R.N. Misra**
—*Sri Premananda Pradhan***

Child labour is a wide spread phenomenon especially in a developing country like India. Poverty and economic inequality are the two major factors invariably related to the incidence of child labour.

Homer Floks, Chairman, United States, National Child Labour Committee defined Child Labour as :

> "Any work by children that interfere with their full physical development, their opportunities for desirable minimum of education or their needed recreation."

CAUSES OF CHILD LABOUR

There are many socio-economic factors responsible for the increase of child labour in India.

1. Poverty

The most important factor favouring child labour is widespread and absolute poverty which forces the parents to send their children to seek employment and to earn money.

2. Growing Illiteracy

In India lower socio-economic groups like Scheduled Caste/ Scheduled Tribes are illiterates. They are ignorant of their

*Dr. Misra, Senior Faculty Member, Science College, Hinjilicut, Orissa.

**Mr. Pradhan is a research scholar.

future and of the importance of modern education. They ignore the fact that child labour deprives the children from their chances of vocational training.

3. Cheap Child Labour

Due to Industrialisation and Modern Scientific Technology, the tendency among the employers is, to secure profit. Since profit is the main objective of the employers, they prefer children as a source of cheap labour and they can be exploited as they lack capability of organising themselves in a trade union.

4. Absence of Family Allowance Scheme

In India, unlike other developing countries, there is a conspicuous absence of schemes for family allowances. So that the prevalance of child labour is, by and large, a problem of poor and destitute families. The poor parents push their children in the job.

THE GRIM STATISTICS ON CHILD LABOUR

Today India is the home of the largest number of working children. According to 1991 census there were 11.29 million child labour. According to the estimate of ILO (1996) there were 12.67 million full time child labour and 10.50 million marginal child labour, found working in different organised and unorganised sectors.

The National Statistical Survey's (NSS) 32nd round (1977-78) estimated child workers in the age group of 5 and 14 years being 16.25 million in 1978. During 1983 the planning projected the number of child workers as 17.4 million.

CHILD LABOUR IN ORISSA

A survey conducted by the Orissa Government has found that 2,15,222 children were employed in various works. It was found that 23,761 children were employed in hazardous establishments, while 1,92,461 children were employed in the non-hazardous establishments. The survey showed that the districts in the coastal belt of the state had less child labourers. For example, Jagatsinghpur had only 412, Sundargarh 871 and

Puri 937 child labourers while the tribal/adivasi districts of Nawarangapur had the highest 32,684 child labourers.

CHILD LABOUR IN HAZARDOUS OCCUPATIONS

The data relating to the nature and extent of child labour in India is simply mind-boggling. Child workers can be seen in almost all parts of the country performing a variety of jobs.

1. A report in the pioneer said that in Ferozabad in Uttar Pradesh more than, 40,000 children labourers are employed in glass industries. The child labourers who have never seen a school, draw molten glass from the furnances for making bracelets and glassware. The report also stated that child workers in the glass industry operate in front of the furnance, where temperature goes up to 1600 degree celsius. Many of them due to harsh working environment, get physically and mentally scared and suffer from chronic illness, destroyed eye-sight, physical stunting and in many cases, even premature deaths.
2. Sivakasi (in Tamil Nadu) is notorious for employing child labour in highly hazardous small scale match and fireworks factories.
3. More than 10 lakh children work in brickpits, stone quarries and other hazardous industries in the banks of the Ganges.
4. Child labour, which so far means exploitation of children in industries and other work places, has now consumed a more sinister form. In Mumbai and Goa for example, "pleasure packages" or sex with children are available.
5. A recent survey conducted by the Shramik Vidyapith of Surat found that around 1,800 Children, under age 14 yrs. were engaged in the hazardous Diamond Cutting Industries.
6. The prevalance of child labour is noticed in the unorganised, informal, and unregulated sectors of the

economy. The unorganised sector accounts for a whole army of child labour working as domestic servants, helpers or assistants in hotels, way side shops, canteens and helpers at construction sites, engaged in breaking stones, unloading goods, etc. Employed children are noticeable in wood carving works, mining sector, beedi making, etc.

The unhygienic working conditions in several jobs expose children to various kinds of health hazards due to the extensive use of chemicals and poisonous substances in industries and pollutants discharged by them. Long hours of working in such conditions obviously endanger the children's physical health and mental growth leading to occupational health problems. The occupational health problems can be illustrated in the following table :

Occupational Health Hazards

Sl. No.	*Occupations*	*Diseases spread*
1.	Match Sticks	Burns of serious type, strain in lifting heavy objects.
2.	Stone mines/ Slate industry	Silicosis.
3.	Carpet Industry	Poisoning by colours/dyes serious ailments of lungs by dust and fibers.
4.	Beedi Industry	Nasal problem, headache, poisoning by nicotine, eye problems and poor eye sight.
5.	Glass Industry	Decrease in longevity due to temperature and dust in environment.
6.	Lock Industry Brass Industry	Asthma, Severe headache, T.B. etc.
7.	Balloon Industry	Heart attack.

The above table reveals that child labourers working in hazardous occupations like carpet making, matches, brass-ware, locks, pottery, gems, etc. contract various diseases like

T.B., skin disorders, burn injuries, silicosis, etc. Besides, children who work with dangerous machines, chemicals and furnances with high temperature run the risk of getting involved in accidents. Since they lack opportunities of education and recreational facilities their social integration becomes difficult.

COMMISSION AND LEGAL ACTS ON CHILD LABOUR

Various commissions have been appointed by the Government of India to study and suggest regarding the problem and eradication of child labour.

1. Royal Commission of Labour, 1929
2. The Labour Investigation Committee, 1944
3. The National Commission on Labour, 1966
4. Gurupada Swamy Committee on Child Labour, 1966
5. Sarat Mehta Committee on Child Labour, 1986

Besides, various Acts have been enacted :

1. Child Labour Prohibition and Regulation Act, 1986
2. The Factories Act, 1982
3. Indian Mines Act, 1923
4. Plantation Labour Act, 1931
5. Motor Transport Workers Act, 1961
6. Beedi and Cigar Workers Condition and Employment Act, 1966 etc.

Article 24 of the Indian Constitution says :

"No child below the age of 14 years shall be employed to work in any factory or mine or be engaged in any hazardous employment."

It is indeed disheartening to note that despite a strong legal and Constitutional backing to curb this massacre, the problems continue to grow. Therefore, some suggested policy measures should be adopted.

SUGGESTED POLICY MEASURES

1. Provisions for providing education for children be made top most priority.
2. The make people aware of the evils of child labour, full use of all means of mass communication such as Doordarshan, Akashvani, Press, Folk Dances, Local Organisations such as village panchayats must be active.
3. There must be severe punishment through legal means to those who violate the Child Labour Act.
4. People must boycott those goods which are produced by child labour.
5. NGO's must involve in various policies and programmes of the Govt. to eradicate the menace of child labour.

To sum up, the practice of child labour is economically unsound, psychologically disastrous and physically as well as morally degrading and harmful for any society. Since, they lack opportunities of education and recreational facilities their social integration becomes difficult. Therefore, it must be rooted out immediately.

REFERENCES

1. Child labour need for new social revolution. Dwarakanath, Dr. H.D. Kurukshetra March, 1999.
2. Sinha, Shantha, Child Labour Kurukshetra, June, 2000.
3. Kurukshetra, March, 1999, p. 17.
4. Kurukeshtra, December, 1998, p. 44.
5. *Ibid.*
6. Civil Services Chronicle, Sept., 1995.
7. Kurukshetra, Dec., 1998, p. 44.
8. *Ibid.*
9. Kurukshetra, March, 1999, p. 20
10. Civil Service Chronicle, Sept., 1995.

7

Silent Cry of Every Child : Abolish Child Labour

—*M. Irshadun Nabi**
—*Sayeda Begum***

"Every new born child proclaims to the world
That God is not desperate with man..."
—*R.N. Tagore*

If we cannot make his future then what right have we to mar it?

Just as the world enters the new millennium, it is time to take stock of our position and progress in the domain of "Child Labour", which is the most comprehensive issue encompassing almost every aspect of the civilized society. Child labour is a global phenomenon having its origin in historical times. The main reason for its growing importance is the fact that almost one-third of the world population comprises 'children'.

'Children', the most precious assets of any nation are the future hope and glory of the country. The progress and prosperity of any nation could be evident from its healthy, promising and dynamic children. Therefore, they deserve to be cared protected and maintained for posterity. Moreover, they makeup an important component of the social structure and are the potential future carriers of culture. Therefore, the

*P.G. Department of Law, Berhampur University, Berhampur, Orissa, 760007.

**Lingaraj Law College, Berhampur, Orissa, 760010.

concept of social justice cannot be conceived without proper justice to children. But, the reality is something different and horrifying. These decorated words on a 'child's life' have lost their significance in the real life of a child.

In India, according to various enactments and legislations, a child belongs to the age-group of five to fourteen years. And, 'child labour' means the employment of children (Five to Fourteen years of age) in gainful occupations that may be injurious to their physical, mental, moral and social development. India is one of the most unfortunate developing countries in the world, having one of the highest percentage of child labour, as high as 25 percent of world's working children are found in India. Child labour contributes significantly to the Indian economy, *i.e.;* 20 percent of GNP.

CAUSES OF CHILD LABOUR

In the underdeveloped and developing countries a formidable population lies below the poverty line. They are not able to arrange for themselves even one square meal a day. Extreme poverty also causes an increase in population. In fact, population and poverty are directly proportional to each other. Ignorance among the masses coupled with poverty makes the family big in its size. In such a situation, where the breadwinner of the family is not capable of looking after his own requirements, what care can he take of his children? How can he protect them from exploitation? How will he secure for them their basic rights? In fact, poverty plays a prime role in diverting a child's route from good schooling and education, to a poor work atmosphere which often costs him his health, snatching away his smiles, innocence and thus hampering the growth of his physical, moral and intellectual capabilities. We should remember here that every child's loss of health and growth is a great loss for the society and the nation as well.

The fields employing children include agriculture, fishing, plantation, manufacturing, maintenance, construction and transport industries, trade and such other services. Most of our export industries like carpet, brassware, and diamond etc; are based on child labour. The recent industrial development in the era of globalisation, has witnessed drastic changes in the nature of work performed by children. Today, children are weaned from their families to work in hazardous industries of the unorganized sectors. From the trade angle, economy is the most important reason giving rise to the problem of child labour.

The various incentives for employing children are as follows :

- If children are employed they are given much lower wages in comparison to their adult counterparts and this ensures low cost of production.
- It is easy to train children since they can learn faster than adults.
- They work honestly and never skip work.
- Their nimble fingers are capable of doing delicate work much faster and with more accuracy.
- Children are more efficient especially in repetitive jobs due to their better concentration power.
- Another important reason of employing children is that, they never create any sort of disturbance in the form of strikes and lockout so, the chances of labour unrest are less. The more the child labour, less is the industrial problems and more the efficiency of an industrial unit.

CHILD LABOUR AND INDIAN CONSTITUTION

The Indian Constitution was drafted almost at the same time as the "Universal Declaration of Human Rights", was adopted and the framers of the Indian Constitution were influenced by the concept of "Human Rights". The Indian Constitution guarantees most of the human rights in two parts. Part *(iii)* of the Constitution provides for legally enforceable or justiciable rights whereas Part *(iv)* of the Constitution casts a duty upon the State to direct its policy towards securing a safe environment for children so that they are not forced by economic necessity to accept avocations unsuited to their age or strength.

As child labour is a socio-economic problem it is generally considered that child labour stems from the evil roots of illiteracy, ignorance, low wages, unemployment, low standard of living, etc. Lack of educational facilities is one of the major causes responsible for the persistence of child labour. The roots of the problem of child labour are hidden in the socio-economic environment of India.

In India, there is actually no law, prohibiting children's participation in jobs. Also there is, no proper constitutional provision for the elimination of child labour. Even the Child Labour Prohibition & Regulation Act, 1986, has extended only a few facilities in the name of certain provisions and has in fact legitimized child labour.

EFFORTS TO PREVENT CHILD LABOUR

The need for providing protection and safeguards to children has first been felt since the Geneva Declaration of the Rights of the Child, 1924 and was later recognized in the Universal Declaration of Human Rights, 1948 and in the statutes of specialized agencies of the U.N.O. Article 25 (2) of the Universal Declaration of Human Rights, 1948, provides that "Motherhood and childhood are entitled to special care and assistance. All children, whether born in or out of wedlock shall enjoy the same social protection". Article 26(1) states that every one has a right to education and it shall be free at least in the elementary and fundamental stages. Needless to say, a solid step has been taken through the Declaration of the Rights of the Child, 1959 that aims at providing the child with a happy childhood that will be enjoyed for his own good and for the good of the society. A major milestone was achieved in 1889, which marked the 30th anniversary of the 1959 Declaration of the Rights of the Child and the 10th anniversary of the International Year of Child. Further, the efforts of International Labour Organization (ILO), in the form of its Conventions and Recommendations, in this regard, are highly applaudable.

CONVENTION NO. 138

The Minimum Age Convention which provides that a ratifying State must pursue a national policy with a dual aim; effectively abolishing child labour, and raising progressively the minimum age for admission to employment or work to a level consistent with the fullest physical and mental development of young persons. Though in general the basic minimum age prescribed is 15 yrs. for developing countries, like India, it is fixed at 14 yrs. As many as 102 countries have ratified this Convention.

A recent development of prohibiting child labour is Convention No. 182, Worst forms of child labour, 1999, which stipulates that the ratifying States must initiate immediate and effective measures to secure as a matter of urgency, the prohibition and elimination of the worst forms of child labour. This comprises : *(a)* all forms of slavery, *(b)* using, procuring and offering of a child for prostitution, *(c)* using, procuring and offering of a child for trafficking of drugs, *(d)* work, which is likely to harm the health safety and morals of a child.

ABOLITION OF CHILD LABOUR

Child labour is undoubtedly a sin, a crime perpetrated against the lives of innocent little children. There can be no justification for denying the opportunities of self-development to the children in this age of abundance. Even after making formidable efforts to curb child labour we are unable to check it. Further, in spite of large-scale investment in child labour rehabilitation projects the results have not been encouraging. Though many child labour projects are working towards the elimination of this problem they have not been able to make significant inroads.

In order to tackle the problem of child labour effectively, we will have to formulate immediately, such a child labour policy, which not only can give the child proper education but also provide requisite skill which can fetch him his much needed livelihood. As we all know that poverty and uncontrolled population growth (which in turn is driven by poverty) are the two main causes of child labour, therefore, steps should be taken first to eliminate poverty. To make this possible the NGOs, Local Self Governments, Media, Social Activists, Educationists, Trade Unions, Human Right Organizations, International Institutions like ILO, UNICEF, and World Bank etc; should join hands to create awareness among the parents, teachers and all those who are responsible for the plight of children.

The parents will have to be educated about the ill effects of such labour on the physical and mental health of their wards and the resultant loss of productivity in future leading to a still greater deprivation and poverty. They should also be motivated to give up their present short-term gains for future long-term gains of higher productivity and efficiency of educated youth.

Young people are the pillars of our nation. They are the pride of our country, society and family. Therefore, for the proper growth and development of such precious assets we need to give a good beginning right from the childhood. It is the obligation of every generation to ensure proper upbringing of children who will be the citizens of tomorrow. Every society, therefore, must devote full attention to ensure that children are properly cared for and brought up in a proper atmosphere where they can receive adequate training, education and guidance for their self-development.

Hear this silent cry of every newborn baby :

"Give me the flame, I'll grow up to
be a fire and lighten the whole world."

Undoubtedly, child labour is a complex issue and therefore requires complimentary strategies, continuous involvement of all sections of civil society. So, let us all try in our own little big way to add to spark and keep the flame always burning bright, to preserve the little ones' innocence and bring smiles on their faces forever.

8

A Child Development Project Officer

—*Prof. S.N. Jena*

Alice said—"I have been in many gardens before, but none of the flowers could talk"

"Put your hands down and feel the ground", said the Tigerlily, "then you will know why."

Alice did so. "It is very hard", she said, "but I do not see what that has to do with it."

The Tigerlily said, "in most gardens, they make the beds too soft—so that flowers are always asleep."

(The Garden of live flowers—Alice's Adventures in Wonderland—Lewis Carroll.)

By virtue of our commitment to welfarism we have included the mosaic. But our funds are at low ebb, so selective programmes are being conducted. Take for example, in schools where the children get their three rupees, an officer makes public visit and gives the need children the required succour. So also the problems of child labour.

The problems are so deep and varied and that too in a court, which is struggling hard to develop. One gets bewildered to think of the goal. Take for example a poor rickshaw pulier taking few bags of cement bags and to help him at places of ups and downs he takes his ten year old son. What can be done to put the boy in child development programme? Or we find boys and girls, five or six years old, following the mother who is searching slums for a piece of iron or plastic.

But it does not mean that one should abandon these attempts at development. Co-ordination and integration of these different projects will help us a long way. In stead of being a child labour officer or a child development officer, if we have one child development officer to tackle with the problems simultaneously the task will be easier. We will put the matter in a concrete form.

A child development project officer will find, from the beginning of the schooling of a child, his family background, his financial condition and his aspiration and lastly his capacity to rise higher and higher on the ladder of general education.

We asked a petty contractor why he has engaged a band of child workers (boy between 14 and 16 years). His reply was—"Such workers are very active and that too, when their mothers and sisters are working in the same place. Secondly, they pick up work and are anxious to work more and earn more. Thus economically, these employees are better." He added, "Sir, at the age of 13 I joined a band of workers under a contractor and now I am a petty contractor at the age of 33. And I am able to execute heavy buildings". These young workers learn while they work as they have no training place for them, so they earn and they learn. How can they be prevented from avocation?

Many of these workers, get spoiled when they, in bad company, get to the habit of drinking wine or country liquor. A carpenter, who has began his earning life, also at the age of 14, told us why he was suffering along with his family, now he gets no work because of his bad habit of gulping wine. Our number is increasing. Can we totally prevent child labour. In villages, all the members of the family go to their field. In urban areas—this is not plausible. Many workers come from the rural areas either they remain away or they travel up and down.

Child labour is detectable to us, the now humanists. But it cannot be absolutely eradicated. (For example, in certain families girls are needed to take care of the bobies etc. So also in certain cases boy-cooks are needed.) Can our Government do in accordance with law any substantial change in the process using child labour for one's own benefit?

Pupils who are above 5 years become aware of their position—poor or rich does not matter. But they cannot express out their feeling. In the primary school stage dignity of labour, dignity of living and dignity of social status should be instilled into the pupils, not by force or compulsion. We do not mean to say that the present set up the teachers in the primary or secondary stage do not tell these points to the pupils but the lacuna is that the premium is not put on this aspect and so this remains as a neglected one. Whether industry department or labour department or education department, take care of the schools, an authority should periodically visit these places and find out how things are going on and whether the pupils are alert on this score. New appointment is not called for a senior teacher or an existing officer who can be in the set up, can be assigned this duty. He will report from time to time to the inspector of schools and follow up action can be taken up. This will help the pupils to rightly understand the developing situation.

Secondly, much is said on the slum seekers—very young boys and girls made through the nasty slums to get a piece of iron, plastic carrier or a toy etc. It is for us to keep an eye on these immatured kids and advise them and their parents to show them the road to a school. The next important consideration is the utilisation of funds. However small it may be, funds are bound to flow. But the proper utilisation of the same is more arduous tasks. Improper use of funds is a great risk, deception, cheating, fraud and mis-using of the funds is a head-ache at present time. It may be from Government or from foreign beneficial organisation or from donations, money is to be properly used—used for the development of the children. Strict vigilance is necessary in such cases. In the name of helping the children of poverty, money may be spent otherwise. Adult vakils, who have neglible legal work, may come forward to have such an organisation and think of making money. Good men who have the sense of dedication for public benefit work, should form a voluntary organisation to help these children to develop. In the case of Bengal, we find many such organisations. Not that we do not have in Orissa, but a lot. The spate of private colleges their results to keep us awake in the dark nights in thinking of the future. If you submit a true report on such colleges, you will fall victim to the watch of the organisations.

In brief, what we want to say is this—a development project officer to co-ordinate and show the right patch is a necessity. As a matter of fact, a department is necessary calling together all such enterprises together from labour, education etc. Call him a child development project officer or any technical officer.

Voluntary organisations may step in with a good purpose—but not for a bad goal. In the garden of humanity, these children—call them Tigerlily, rose or whatever name is suitable—are to flower out. Let them not welt away in utter helplessness.

Lastly, let us not put the manure on the top of the tree, but put it at the root. So a nation grows excellent and great if we take care of the foundation. The children' whether rich or poor, provide the foundation and if we neglect them we are in a helpless manner needed in the nation. Today's slums searchers, if picked up and nurtured, may become noble and great men of tomorrow. We the adults, live for them and they make us live longer. No question of this or that department to think of their full and total growth for the country. The should be healthy, educated and qualified for the nation.

9

The Menace of Child Labour—An Observation

*—Dr. R.N. Misra**

*—Mr. Roopesh K. Misra***

INTRODUCTION

During the present era, the Child Labour has come to lime light for discussion widely in many circles. Voluntary organisations, the Governments, International organisations, journalists, and other Media persons have been highlighting the situation of working children in the country. Children are the assets of the society. It is the primary responsibility of the society to nurture them through various phases of their development in order to ensure a better quality of life to them for the growth and development of the country. Millions of children come to the streets for a hand-full of rice. The working of children in hazardous occupation is a fire-fighting problem of the present day. It is the duty of all to look into, how to overcome this problem.

WHO IS A CHILD LABOUR

According to Section 2*(ii)* of the Child Labour (Prohibition and Regulation) Act 1986, a Child has been defined as a person who has not yet completed his/her fourteenth year of age.

The Hon'ble Supreme Court of India, in their judgment on Child labour in a writ petition (c) No. 465 of 986 M.C.

*Dr. Mishra, Senior Faculty Member, Dept. of Commerce, S.C. College, Hinjilicut,

**Sri Roopesh K. Misra, a research scholar.

Mehta Vs. State of Tamil Nadu and others dated 10.12.1996, has given certain directions for identification of child labour in hazardous work and following and following actions are to be initiated thereafter.

1. The manner in which the children, working in hazardous occupations, are to be withdrawn from hazardous work and be rehabilitated.
2. Payment of compensation amounting to Rs. 20,000 be paid by the employer to every such child.
3. An adult member of the family should be employed in place of a child.
4. A fund should be created in each district to see the benefits of child labour, who are on hazardous occupation, named "Child Labour Rehabilitation-Cum Welfare Fund" under the Chairmanship of Dist. Collector.

According to UNICEF, any child out of School is a child labour. But in terms of priority of action, it is imperative to abolish the most exploitative and most intolerable forms of child labour as a first priority. In the context of exploitation, UNICEF has given a comprehensive formulation in its attempt while defining child labour :

1. Starting fulltime work at too early an age.
2. Working too long within or outside the family and unable to attend School.
3. Working in a unhealthy and dangerous occupations.
4. Too much responsibility at too early an age.
5. Inadequate remuneration for working outside the family as in the case of child workers in carpet weaving industry.

A WORKING CHILD

A working child is a child in the age group of 5 to 14 years, who is doing labour, either paid or unpaid at outside the family having no specific time for work. The children who are out-of-school, are taken for granted as child labourers in one form or other. It does not make any distinction between children working in the so-called hazardous industries and children working as part of family labour. If children are working 12-14 hours per day alongwith their parents, at the cost of their education, their situation is similar to that of children working for other employers. In fact, particularly girl children are engaged by the parents specially by elder family members for more then 12 hours so that she can able to work at her in-laws house after marriage.

CHILDREN IN HAZARDOUS OCCUPATIONS

Article 14 of Indian Constitution prescribes that no child under 14 years would be made to work in any factory or a mine or engaged in any other hazardous employment. Article 39 (e) of the constitution directs the Govt. of India to see that the tender age children are not abused and that the parents are not compelled by their economic condition to force their children to work in an unhealthy areas.

As per part 'A' and 'B' of the schedule to the child labour (Prohibition and Regulation) Act, 1986 children have been prohibited to work in certain occupations and processes defined as hazardous. Important hazardous occupation, according to part 'A' include.

1. Transport of passengers, goods or mails by railways.
2. Work in a catering establishment at a railway station. The movement of a child labourer from one platform to another of into or out of a moving train.
3. Any work relating to the construction of a railway station or with any other work where such work is done in close proximity, between railway lines.
4. Work in a port authority within the limits of any port.
5. Work relating to fire work and selling of fire crackers in the shop.

Important items of hazardous occupation under 'B' schedule :

1. Beedi making
2. Carpet weaving
3. Cement manufacture including begging of cement
4. Cloth printing, dyeing and weaving
5. Manufacturing of matches, explosives and fire works
6. Mica-cutting and splitting
7. Shell manufacture
8. Soap manufacture
9. Training
10. Wool clearing
11. Building and construction industry.

List of Industries Involving Hazardous Processes :

Hazardous processes in Industrial Sector is defined in section 2(cb) of factories Act, 1948. These are as follows :

1. Ferrous Metallurgical Industries
2. Coal (including coke) Industries
3. Power generating Industries
4. Fertiliser Industries
5. Petroleum Industries
6. Drug and Pharmaceutical Industries.

Child labourer engaged in hazardous occupations are mostly, found in the organised sector in areas, where people are not aware of their rights. Again poverty, illiteracy, lack of awareness and large family size force the young children to work in the hazardous sectors.

CAUSES AND CONSEQUENCES OF CHILD LABOURER

Problem of child labour is very old and global in character. It is fire fighting exercise of the day. Child labour is the result of exploitation of the weak and poorest sections of the society who are far below the poverty line. When a grown up child is unable to get minimum food for a day for him, due to poor condition of his parent, he cames to the street to work. When a child comes forward to start working, he has no bargain power before his employeer, due to illiterate lack of skill. So he is unable to demand reasonable wages for his work. Working long hours, without proper food, social problems lead to the poor health of the child. Huge debt of the parent, unemployment, social customs backwardness low caste etc. force a grown up child to work. But among all poverty is consider as major problem which forces a child to go for work instead of school.

So, from all the engles it is believed that without poverty erdication child labour cannot be eliminated. The questions that are most often asked me : What will happen to the families of these children if child labour is eradicated? How will poor families survive without the additional income of the children? Unless some steps are taken to improve the standard of living of the parent, the children have to work for the survival of their parents. The parents use their own children as most important asset when all other assets disappear.

SUGGESTIONS

To eliminate child labour to a maximum extent in the developing country like ours, some drastic actions should be taken to improve the scenario. So suggestions are put forth how to improve the working condition of child labour.

1. A door-to-door survey, has to be taken up to identify child labour, both in rural and urban areas and steps should have to be initiated to build up a socio-economic profile of affected families under the supervision of state and Central Govt.
2. From the available data, a plan has to be prepared on long term basis to provide proper/adequate resources to make the parent of the children self sufficient in food and clothing.
3. From the data, potential child should be separated and they should be given proper education facilities by the Govt. and other agencies as free of cast.

4. Punishment should be given to the employers, who are torturing the children physically, mentally and economically.
5. Some effective policies must be framed so that the child should became free at his own desire.

REFERENCES

1. Bhandari, J., "Child Labour : The Challenges Ahead", *Yojana,* Vol. 44, New Delhi, Sept. 2000.
2. Burra N., Child Labour in India, Oxford University Press, 1995.
3. Butterflies, 'My Name is To-day', Children News, Vol. II, No. 2, April-June, New Delhi.
4. Special Survey Reports, Govt. of India, Bhubaneswar, No. 16.
5. Govt. of India, All India Census Report, 1991, New Delhi.
6. Misra, R.N., Rural Development and Population. Anmol Publications (P) Ltd., New Delhi, 2002.

10

Child Labour : An Unsolved Problem

—*Sri Sudarsan Jena**
—*Sri Kedar Nath Bisoyee***

Even after fity-five years of independence and irrespective of several laws passed for the prohibition of Chid Labour in various countries including India, more than 370 million children of our country have been struggling to break the chains of bondage and employment in multi-dimensional hazardous and non-hazardous occupations.

A broad picture containing the statistical data of child labour in the global context have been presented in table 10.1 & 10.2. It has been estimated that out of total child labourers of the world, 80% are found in Asia, 58% in South Asia, and more than 30% in India. Thus, India contributes to about a third of Asia's Child Labour force and a fourth of the world's working children.[1]

The experimental surveys by the ILO's Bureau of Statistics indicate that an estimated 120 million children between the ages of 5 and 14 yrs. work full time in developing countries. The number rises to 250 million if secondary activity is also included. But out of the estimated 250 million child labour in the world, Asia has the largest number of child workers with 153 million (61%). Whereas in Africa and in Latin America, these figures are 80 million (32) and 17 million (7%) respectively. In relatives terms, however, Africa comes first in the

*Lecturer in Economics, Adivasi College, Balliguda, Kandhamal (Orissa).

**Project Director, National Child Labour Project, Malkangiri (Orissa).

Table 10.1. Economically Active Child Population in the South Asian Countries

Country	*Children*			*Male Children*			*Female children*		
	Age group	*Active population*	*Activity rate*	*Total population*	*Active population*	*Activity rate*	*Total population*	*Active population*	*Activity rate*
Bangladesh	10-14	56,677,000	33.3	9,064,000	3,430,000	37.8	7,992,000	2,247,000	28.1
India	5-14	11,285,349	5.4	109,366,794	6,189,834	5.7	100,619,836	5,095,515	5.1
Indonesia	10-14	1,922,810	8.0	12,162,317	1,130,221	9.3	11,790,943	792,589	6.7
Nepal	10-14	531,835	22.9	1,209,803	218,979	18.1	1,117,483	312,856	28.0
Pakistan	10-14	1,906,000	11.6	8,866,000	1,467,000	16.5	7,633,000	439,000	5.8
Srilanka	10-14	28,615	1.8	831,348	18,628	2.2	802,989	9,987	1.2

Source : ILO (1997) Year Book of Labour Statistic.

Table 10.2. Incidence of Child Labour, ***Age Group (10—14) Percentage***

Country/Regions	*1980*	*1997*
Bangladesh	35	29
India	21	13
Nepal	56	44
Pakistan	23	17
Srilanka	4	2
South Asia	23	16
Sub-Saharan Afrika	35	30
Latin America	13	9
East Asia & Pacific	27	5
Middle East & North Africa	14	5
Europe and Central Asia	3	1
World	20	13

Source : World Bank's World Development Indicators, 1999.

percentage of children participating in economic activities, with an estimated 41 per cent of the total number of children aged between 5 and 14 yrs compared to 22 per cent in Asia and 17 per cent in Latin America.

CHILD LABOUR IN SOUTH ASIA COUNTRIES

In Asia, where 61 per cent of the world population of working children live, imbalances manifesto in terms of percentage of child population-economic activities. The activity rate* among children in South Asia ranged from 1.8 per cent to 33.3 per cent. (Table No. 10.1 & 10.2).

If we look at the statistics on economically active child, child population in the South Asian countries, India dominates in absolute terms with 11.2 million children in the age group of 5 to 14 years participating in economic activities, followed by Bangladesh with 5.6 million children labouring in the age group of 10 to 14 yrs. In relative terms, Bangladesh has an

*Percentage of children participating in economic activities.

abnormally high percentage (33.3) of all its children in the age group of 10-14 yrs. participating in economic activities followed by Nepal with 22.9 per cent. Pakistan with 11.6 per cent, Indonesia with 8 per cent and India with an activity rate of 5.4 per cent.

In the context of male and female distribution of child labour in South Asian countries, Bangladesh with 37.8 per cent of activity rate for male children was followed by Nepal (18.1%) and Pakistan (16.5%). It is 5.7 per cent of male child population which is in economic activity in case of India. But sharp variations can be found in the employment of female child in these countries. While Bangladesh and Nepal have the same percentage (28.0), it is 5.8 per cent in Pakistan and 5.1 per cent in India. More than 80% of the working children in Asia belong to the rural areas and work in the unorganised primary sector of the economy. They enter the labour market to help poverty affected families, to repay long standing family debts, because of sudden death of bread-winner of the family or sanctions when they run away from the families because of personal or caste exploitation. No single cause can be identified, as it is inherent in the vicious circle of poverty, un-employment and lack of income or income generating assets.

Child labour in rural areas is not considered as exploitative, since it is carried out under the protective guidance of parents or elders in the family. Many consider it a process of socialisation and the only means of acquiring the necessary skills required for survival in the given environment. It is believed that such child labour develops the confidence, self result and personality of young workers and prepares them to take-over the responsibility from elders of continuing the traditional family-occupations as they grow into adults.

The elimination of child labour has been the aim of numerous Government or voluntary initiatives in various parts of the world. Experiences have exhibited that these projects and programmes encounter problems associated with the reality faced by child labourers' families. Thus, there is an imperative need to replace a child's income or labour contribution to the household and to encourage attendance in school of poor children by providing economic incentives either in cash or in kind.[2] It is lamenting that despite plethora of acts and legislations, child labourers are working under exploitative conditions. Presently the act :

(i) bans the employment of children—*i.e.* who have not completed their 14th year, in specified occupations and processes;

(ii) lays down a procedure to decide modifications to the schedule of banned occupations or processes;

(iii) regulates the conditions of work of children in employment where they are not prohibited from working;

(iv) lays down enhanced penalties for the employment of the children in violation of the provisions of Act, and other acts which forbid the employment of children; and

(v) brings about uniformity in the definition of 'Child' in related laws. Child labour (Prohibition and Regulation) Act, 1986 is limited in its approach as it has given no distinction between work that is generally hazardous and that specifically so far growing child. This is imperative because even so called non-hazardous jobs can prove dangerous :

—Accidents are more likely to happen due to immaturity, physical and mental fatigue.

—Children are subject to physical abuse.

—Excessive hours of work are demanded from children.

—Dangerous jobs like creeping under machinery are given to children because of their size.

—More dirty work is given to children.

—Posture related problems are more hazardous for growing children.

—Children in prostitution are exposed to AIDS and ill-equipped for its prevention.[3]

(Reference Kit on child labour for Media persons)

Table 10.3. Child Labour in India

Industry	*Location*	*Total Workers*	*Child workers*	*%of child workers to total workers*
1	*2*	*3*	*4*	*5*
Slate pencil	Mandsaur, Madhya Predesh	12000	1000	8.3
Slate	Markpur, Andhra Pradesh	15000	3750	25
Diamond cutting	Surat, Gujarat	100000	15000	15
Agate-cutting	Cambay, Gujarat	30000	Not known	—
Gem polishing	Jaipur, Rajasthan	60000	13600	22.6
Powerloom	Bhiwandi, Maharashtra	300000	15000	5
Cotton Hosiery	Trippur, Tamil Naidu	30000	8000	33.3
Carpet weaving	Mirjapur-Bhadohi, U.P.	200000	150000	75
Carpet weaving	Jammu & Kashmir	400000	100000	25
Carpet weaving	Rajasthan	30000	12000	40
Lock making	Aligarh, U.P.	80000	7000	8.7
Lock making	Uttar Pradesh	90000	10000	11.1
Pottery	Khurja, U.P.	20000	5000	25
Brass ware	Moradabad, U.P.	150000	40000	20.6
Match	Sivakasi	Not known	45000	—
Glass	Firozabad, U.P.	200000	50000	25

(Contd.)

(Contd.)

1	*2*	*3*	*4*	*5*
Silk and silk products textile	Varanasi, Uttar Pradesh	11900	4409	37
Textile	Varanasi, Uttar Pradesh	3512	1108	31.5
Knives	Rampur, U.P.	Not known	3000	—
Handicrafts	Jammu & Kashmir	90000	26478	29.2
Silk weaving	Bihar	Not known	10000	—
Brocade and Zari	Varanasi and other centers	Not known	300000	—
Brick-klin	West Bengal	Not known	35000	—
Beedi	India	3275000	327500	10
Circus Industry	40 major circuses	—	12% of the entire Labour strength	—

Source : Neera Burra, Born to work : Child Labour in India, ppxxii-xxiv, as quoted by Supreme Court of India in M.C. Mehta v. State of Tamil Naidu, 1996(6) SCC 756 at pp. 763-764.

The extent child labour is so alarming and extensive in Indian context, it can be out-lined in Table 10.3. It is observed that there has been leakages of funds meant for development activities, rural development projects, income & employment intensive projects resulting in increasing poverty and child labour.

There is a need for a well defined action plan which should recognize the importance of awareness campaigns proper surveys, legislative action against employers and welfare schemes for children. Besides, political leaders, NGOs and social activists should make concerted efforts so that poverty—the root cause of child expioitation can be removed.[4]

Moreover, corruption and misutilisation of funds must be prohibited by constitutional amendments and effective legislation so as to make a frontal attack on poverty and child labour in Indian States.

REFERENCES

1. Sheikh Ajaz Ahmed, Child Carpet Weavers of Kashmir, Social Welfare, November, 2000, p. 14.
2. K. Suman Chandra & M.M. Basha, Social Dimensions of Child Labour, Social Welfare, November, 2000, p. 3.
3. Ahuja, Daman, Politics of Child Labour, Social Welfare, November, 2001, p. 14-15.
4. Tripathy, S.N., Migrant Child Labour in India, Mohit Publications, New Delhi, 1997.

11

Child Labour in Fishing Community

—R.P. Sarma

The factory system of production, production at particular location operated by the paid workers—daily, monthly or annual wage basis—emerged towards the end of 18th century in the western countries on modern lines of management. During the last two centuries workers wages have been standardised and the amount of minimum wages have been controlled by the state. With coming up of the trade unions in the mid nineteenth century more and more benefits were provided to the workmen in industries including job security in the factory sector.

Developed countries with the development of social system and educational facilities in the middle of the nineteenth century, the national governments in order to provide social justice to the people several legal measures have been adopted to protect the rights of children, of which the most important one is right to education. All over the world the states expressed grave concerns over illiteracy, which is considered as most important variable for the socio economic development of a society. In the developing economics the rapid growth of population along with slow growth rate of literacy has been regarded the two most important bottleneck for economic development.

Eradicating illiteracy is a Herculean task in the developing countries. There are two important reasons for this among others, one is economic and other is societal. The main economic cause is poverty. It is the main cause of illiteracy as the poverty stricken families compel their children to take up petty jobs to supplement the family income, instead of sending them to the school to learn some alphabets.

The social cause is not less crucial one. The families who are above poverty line due to narrow social outlook prevent their children to attend school, or withdraw their children after one or two primary classes. These families are not interested to send their children to the school because of these actors :

1. Investing on education is wastage of money or what the economist call it as unproductive expenditure. Instead of spending money on education they prefer to spend it on some daily consumer goods for the betterment of the children.
2. It is feared that once the children are educated they leave the family for other jobs and would not help the family in their traditional profession. Once educated they are reluctant to work in the traditional professional work in the family.
3. As far as the girl children are concerned it is traditionally believed that there is no necessity of education. They are given marriage at an early age to get rid of the responsibility of the parents. Before marriage they are also engaged in family work or in the formal industries.

According to the legal definition in India, engaging children below 14 years of age is termed as child labour. The organisations employing child labour can be divided into two categories :

(a) *Child Labour in Organised Sector :* In these sectors employment of child labour is comparatively low; it is confined to certain industries. Here the employment of child labour can be easily detracted and legal restriction can be imposed.

(b) *Child Labour in Unorganised Sector :* Child labour is wide spread in this sector. Among others this sector includes agriculture, mining, fishing, hand loom industry etc. in the rural sector and tailoring, cycle repairing, small hotels etc. in the urban sector.

According to the nature of job the employment of child labour in the unorganised sector can further be divided into two parts :

(a) Employment of child labour in the family traditional professional jobs. The child is unconsciously involves himself in the family work with the parents, even though he is not paid any separate wages for the work; it is treated the combined work of the family. As apart of the family member the children work there. These include agriculture, fishing, pottery, hand loom clothes etc.

(b) Child labour is engaged in some other jobs under unorganised sector where it is not the traditional family work. Each member of the family may work in different jobs with family members or without the family members participating in it. In road and building construction, domestic servants etc. both adult and children are engaged and usually there is no restriction for the child labour for work.

Classification of industries in which child labour is generally engaged can be shown in a schematic diagram. This is presented in Fig. 11.1.

THE FISHERMAN COMMUNITY

Fishing activity is one of the ancient professional activities of the society. From time immemorial the family members of this community catching and marketing fish from the inland and marine waters. Previously they have been used to the crude traditional methods of fishing but now a day there is sea change in the methods of catching and marketing fish. Now mechanised boats and trawlers and extensively used for fishing on commercial basis.

With the modern development of fisheries the traditional fishermen community dwindled to smaller population as a result of big business houses entered in the fishing activity on a large scale. The fishing companies are prospering with good earnings marketing fish nationally and internationally, but the traditional fishermen community in India could not come out of "hand-to-mouth" situation in the family.

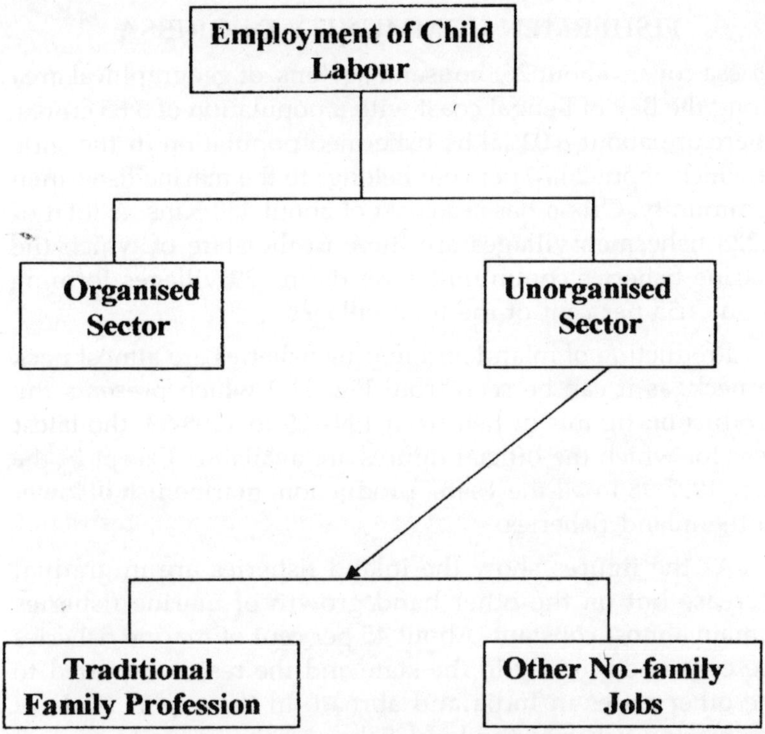

Fig. 11.1. Employment of Child Labour.

The fishermen community is broadly classified into two groups : *(a)* Inland fishermen community and *(b)* Marine fishermen community. The former community catch fish in inland waters such as ponds, tanks and rivers. The latter marine community reside with in about 3 Km. of the sea shore and catch fish from sea. They have tough job than the inland fishermen. Facing all types of hazards and calamities in the sea they brave the activity of fishing sometimes in the worst condition inside the sea risking life. Of course now-a-days marine fish, especially prawns and lobsters are being cultivated in the ponds, but they are of limited magnitude. Since the marine fishermen community live only in the coastal land their population is far lower than the inland fishermen community. Their economic condition and standard of living is lower to the inland fishermen community.

FISHERMEN COMMUNITY IN ORISSA

Orissa covers about 26 thousand sq. kms. of geographical area along the Bay of Bengal coast with a population of 3.65 crores. There are about 8.02 lakhs fishermen population in the state of which about 20.70 per cent belongs to the marine fishermen community. Orissa has sea coast of about 480 Kms. A total of 7,228 fishermen villages are there in the state of which the marine fisheries communities reside in 329 villages forming about 4.55 per cent of the total villages.

Production of inland and marine fisheries are almost neck to neck, as it can be seen from Fig. 11.2 which presents the production figures of fish from 1994-95 to 1998-99, the latest year for which the official figures are available. Except in the year 1997-98 in all the years' production, marine fish is lower to the inland fisheries.

As the figures show the inland fisheries are in gradual increase but on the other hand growth of marine fisheries remain almost constant. About 45 per cent of marine fisheries are consumed locally in the state and the rest is exported to the other states in India and abroad. In the export trade of the marine fisheries the local fishermen community are not benefited even though their roll in fish landing is considerable.

The traditional fishermen community operate non-mechanised boats; and it is found that the number of non-mechanised bots and their catch of fish in the total marine fish production is on declining, which indicates the deteriorated economic condition of the marine fisheries community in Orissa. In the year 1990-91 there were 13,488 non-mechanised boats and their catch in the total marine fish production was about 51.23 per cent. The share of the traditional fish catching

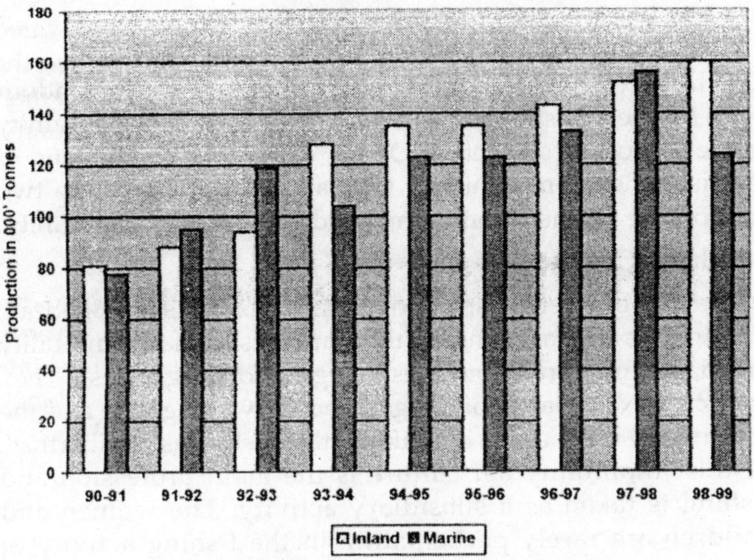

Fig. 11.2. Production of Inland & Marine Fisheries.

declined to about 33.39 per cent by the year 1996-97. But the figures show that productivity of fish catch per boat increased considerably; from about 3 tonnes per boat in the year 1990-91 to about 5 tons per boat in the year 1996-97.

Table 11.1 shows the figures of number of boats, production of fish and per cent of marine fish catch from the year 1990-91 through 1996-97 in support of this.

Table 11.1. Growth of Traditional Boat and Fish Catch

Year	*No. of Boats*	*Production in Tonnes*	*Per cent of catch*
1990-91	13,488	40,066	51.23
1991-92	13,340	39,166	41.22
1992-93	12,180	48,854	40.92
1993-94	9,462	39,206	37.73
1994-95	7,796	45,656	37.15
1995-96	8,557	46,200	37.50
1996-97	8,358	44,569	33.39

*Cuttack includes two districts of Kendra Para and Jagatsinghpur.

THE SAMPLE HOUSEHOLDS

One hundred households have been sampled out on random basis for the investigation of the marine fishermen community in the six coastal districts of Orissa. The ethnic background of the fishermen community of Orissa can be divided into two groups : the northern community and the southern community.

Northern Community

In the four northern districts of Orissa viz., Balasore, Bhadrak, Kendrapara and Jagatsingpur the marine fishermen community are mainly migrants from West Bengal and Bangla Desh. They speak a mixed dialect of Bengali and Oriya language and the community is generally identifying themselves as "Kaibartha". In this community agriculture is the main profession and fishing is taken as a subsidiary activity. The women and children are rarely participating in the fishing activity or marketing of fish. About 50 to 80 percent of these fishermen have no boats of their own and 20 to 30 per cent do not possess any net of their own.

Southern Community

In the two districts of southern coast, the districts of Puri and Ganjam, the majority of the fishermen families are Telugu speaking migrated from Andhra Pradesh centuries back. Most of the villages are nearer the sea shore. Unlike the northern community in the southern part the women and children dominantly participate in the fishing activity especially in marketing and processing of fish. Even though there are sub-casts among these fishermen community they are mainly known as "Nolia".

DEMOGRAPHIC CHARACTERISTICS

These 100 sample families have total population of 564 which comes to 5.64 members per family. The sex ratio is 845 women per 1000 males. The literacy among the community is about 14 per cent, of which female literacy is 9.34 per cent while the male literacy is 17.91 per cent. It is found that there is not a single literate person in the sample families in the district of Puri and Ganjam. In these districts the participation of women in the fishing activity is highest in comparison to the northern coast. In Puri about 96 per cent of females are engaged in the fishing activity while in Ganjam the percentage is about 83.

ANNUAL INCOME OF THE FAMILY

Annual income comes to Rs. 8,900 per family mainly from the fishing activity. Ownership of land is with about 10 per cent of the households and it adds marginally to the annual income earned by the families from the fisheries. The annual income earnings varied from districts to district with a lowest income earning in the district of Ganjam with Rs. 6,100 and highest with Rs. 10,850 in the district of Balasore as the figure shown in Table 11.2.

Table 11.2. Annual Income of the Families

District	*Annual Income*	*Difference From Mean*
Balasore	10,850	+1,950
Cuttack	7,000	–1,900
Puri	9,900	+1,000
Ganjam	6,100	–2,800
Mean	8,900	

It is found from the survey that only 5 per cent of the families posses boats of their own. About 57 per cent of the families have nets of different kind of their own. Another 21 per cent of the families possess both boat and nets that are comparatively with a higher income group. The rest of the 17 per cent does not possess any nets or boats, they work in other's boats as daily wage earners or get a share of the catch with the participating in the fishing operation of the day. They are like "land-less labourer" in agriculture that depends on the daily wages only.

The daily catch of fish is very meagre. About 77 per cent of the families catch daily only 20 Kg. or less than it. Hence the income is very meagre. Depending on the actual quantity and quality of catch the daily earning for the family ranges between Rs. 10 to Rs. 100. During the cyclones and other natural calamities the families go with out any earnings.

CHILD LABOUR IN THE FAMILY

Among the 100 ample families there are 191 children which come to an average of 1.91 children per family, which is lower to the national norm of 2 children per family set by the government of India in their population policy. Of course when 12 families who have no child are excluded the average children per family come to 2.45. Out of the total number of children, 60 children are aged 5 or less than 5 which forms about 31.41 per cent.

Out of the total number of 191 children the number of children in the working age group of 5 to 14 years constitutes 70.68 per cent. In case of female children the working age group children constitutes 68 per cent while from the female children 73.62 per cent are in the working age group. Of the total working group children 26.47 per cent are attending school and partially help the parents in the fishing activities. While among female children 22.39 per cent are attending school.

The number children in the working age group and number of child labour engaged in the family occupation are shown in Fig. 11.3.

In the districts of Cuttack and Puri not a single child has attended the school in the sample fishermen families. In these districts the fishermen community are mainly migrated from Andhra Pradesh. They live in the sea sore itself in small helmets where there are no facilities for schooling. Hence all the children in the working age group have to work in the family profession.

Among the working age group children, excluding the school going children, the rest 102 children work with their family in the different types fishing operations. This indicates that about 75.56 per cent are working as child labour in the family profession. The other children who are going to school are also engaged in the profession as part time helping their parents off the school work.

The district-wise break up of male and female children in

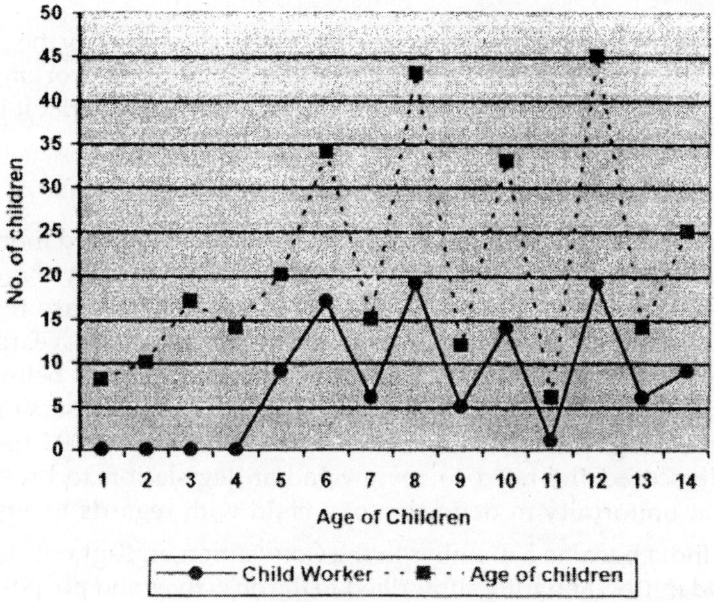

Fig. 11.3. Child Labour among Children.

the working age group and children attending school there off with gender wise is presented in Table 11.3. This indicates that about 74 per cent of boys and 78 per cent of girls work in the family profession of fishing in these marine fishermen community. Among the districts, in two districts of Cuttack and Puri the child labour is cent per cent as no child goes to

Table 11.3. Working Age Group and School Going Children

District	*Working Age Children*		*School Going*	
	Male	*Female*	*Male*	*Female*
Balasore	16	17	5	5
Bhadrak	21	18	6	7
Cuttack*	5	9	0	0
Puri	14	13	0	0
Ganjam	12	10	7	3
Total	68	67	18	15

* Cuttack includes two districts of Kendrapara and Jagatsinghpur.

school from the fishermen families. In two of the northern districts the percentage of child labour to the total working age children is about 65 per cent, while in Ganjam district it is about 55 per cent.

RIGHT OF THE CHILD IN INDIA

India has largest child population in the world estimated more than 38 crores below the age of 18 years. In our country there is no uniformity in the definition of child, in some case the age is taken as 14 but for others it is extended to 18 years. According to the international norm a child is defined below the age of 18. Recently U.N. General Assembly's special session on the "Rights of the Child" held from 8th to 10th 2002 has underscored the need to review Indian legislation to bring about uniformity in definition of a child with regards to age.

India become a member to the Convention on Right of the Child in 1993 and fully subscribed to the objectives and purpose subscribed to the objectives and purpose of the convention realising the rights of the child. However declared that, "those pertaining to the economic, social and cultural rights (of the children) can only progressively implemented...subject to the extent of available resources and with in the framework of international co-operation.

India's first mandatory report to the Right of Child Committee made in March 1997. It described different legal provision made to protect the Rights of the Child and admitted that it is not tractable to prescribe minimum age for admission to each and every area of employment in the country. However the UN Convention realising the legal and administrative difficulties asked India :

1. To adopt a code for children;
2. Effective implementation of existing legislation; and
3. Strengthen the capacity and effectiveness of the national human rights institutions.

CONCLUSION

Protection of economic, social and cultural rights of child is a

Herculean task. But efforts should be made continuously by government and non-governmental organisations towards this end. As analysed above, in the marine fishermen community child labour is 75 per cent among the working age children. In other family traditional industries it extends up to 100 per cent. Instead of legal provisions for the restriction of child labour the preventive checks with regards to improving the economic condition of the people and increasing literacy would be more effective. But this would be a long drawn process.

REFERENCES

Bala, Supriya (1999), *Economics of Marine Fisheries in Orissa,* Unpublished Ph.D. thesis, Berhampur University.

BOBP (1993), *The Impact of Environment on the Fisheries of Orissa,* Rep. 67, Madras.

Government of Orissa (1997), *Hand Book on fisheries Statistics, Orissa 1996-97,* Directorate of Fisheries, Bhubaneswar.

Nayak, A.P. (1992), *Socio-economies of Artisan Marine Fisheries along Ganjam Coast,* OUAT, Rangeilunda.

Sahu, Purushottam (2000). *Environment and Fishermen Community in the District of Ganjam, Orissa,* Unpublished Ph.D. thesis, Berhampur University.

Tietze, U., & Kalavati (1994), *Artisan Marine Fishier Folk of Orissa,* Vidyapuri, Cuttack.

12

Child Labour is a Social Evil—A Look

—*B.C. Mahapatra**

INTRODUCTION

Work is worship—Work alone is God. "Karma" is work and to do work. Physical and Mental energy is utilized. This power to do work *viz.* energy is a constant and goes on transforming from one state to another. The fetus in the mothers womb, made up of 5 elements (Panchamahabhuta) becomes active with the slightest touch of that celestial energy "Atma" and this living organisms gets further energy from food, water, proper rest and a contemnned brain before and after birth. Thus life is nothing but a little bit of energy given to the body structure to do work, both mental and physical to achieve the target. Then what is fate? Why a good student becomes unsuccessful in the final examination and a good player fails to win the match? Here labour is not directly proportional to the result. We can establish this by saying that time did not favour despite of hard labour and sincere efforts. Time (Kala) is the only examiner and unless we satisfy "kala", we cannot be crowned with success. Rich-poor, educated-illiterate classification among men are purely a circumstantial factor only. Irrespective of caste, creed and religion, an innocent lovely tender child is loved by all. He has no friend or foe—a nice created of God—a precious gift .of nature. The environment in which he is born and brought up, the way in which he is further nourished created this difference. The opportunities given to this child differed amenities to grow

*Mr. Mahapatra, Retd. D.E. Telecom, Gandhinagar-3, Berhampur.

up decently blocked. Hence he is poor, illiterate, backward working class individual of the society. This demarcation is manmade and the almighty need not be blamed for this. He is ever impartial and demands duty, small or big from every individual. For him cleaning municipal drain is important as making an atom bomb. Both are equally useful for the society one for good health while the other for tight security. Big men doing small jobs set example for others and advise there is nothing to hate or worry about it. If taken in proper perspective.

Four-caste classification was made in Veda on work analysis basis unlike different departments in Govt. or business organization. A man doing a particular job for generations becomes and expert in that trade and gives wonderful service to society. Brahmins, Khatriyas, Vaisyas and Sudras are inseparable organs of a living society and no limb is ever useless for smooth functioning of the social structure.

LABOUR

Apart from mental labour of enlightened professional physicians, engineers, business magnets coming under rich and literate category, physical labour is divided into 2 classes *viz.* skilled & unskilled. The job skill is gained out of personal experience and interest. These labourers work under the direction of work engineers, supervisors and supervise unskilled work which does not involve any intelligent thinking, mathematical measurements etc. skilled wage ought to be a little more than the unskilled wage and there is nothing to grudge about it. The labourer giving routine manual labour should not feel that he is inferior to his friend in the skilled category and he need not boost up his mind foolishly creating unnecessary unwanted financial shortage and painful wants. Present day wants are due to virtual raise of one's status beyond his earning capacity and getting unnecessary worries to meet the deficit. Some how imitation to upper strata is always painful. Rather a steady look to downward will give mental satisfaction that he is in the middle, much better than the people below him. But alas! This illogical imitation to upper class and consequent mental agony is the route course of all labour crises, agitation strikes. Lockouts in the entire globe, where everything is now money oriented to provide ample luxury to the moral body.

Without exploitation no body can be rich overnight and to stop exploitation several revolutions in industry & agriculture sectors have taken place. Labour union leaders sit in the joint consultation meetings with the owners and sorted out solutions for an amicable settlement of the dispute. Wages and other related facilities like accommodation, medical treatment, bonus etc., granted to workers and their families and both the owner and workers co-exist after meeting their respective vested interests. Production, marketing trade going on as usual labour crisis. Production loss, bankruptcy etc., are dangerous to both the working class as well as the employer. To reduce manual strength, if help of technology his taken to make up the work unnecessary retrenchment, voluntary retirement, dismissal will give immense sorrow and suffering to working class. For their own interest workers should also see the interest of their employers and both should co-exist in a healthy atmosphere.

CHILD LABOUR

Child is ever considered as a valuable gift of God to wanting parents. He is the builder of the future generation. Childhood is a precious period in every life. Tender in body and mind, innocent baby of today in mother's lap grows up walking, speaking, limping, playing up to 5 years. The age group 5-14 is real childhood. Where the child is supposed to get full parental care for building up good health, mind and smartness. He will go to school for educating himself to know the world around him along with his playmates. The teacher has to take full responsibility for good education and character building. Thus he will be made ready to study further and become a full-fledged-enlightened citizen of the society.

India is mainly an agricultural country, where majority of people live in villages. In 1947 independent India had a population of 40 crores where as now it has gone up to 100 crores. Illiteracy is primarily responsible for this population out burst as God fearing innocent rural people took birth control as sin. Further a child was then considered to be asset for wage earning in a poor illiterate rural family of labour class. They never bothered for education of the child. Soon after they attain 5 years. Parents engage their children to graze cattle and other domestic animals. At the age of 10-12 children work with their parents in the field and earn half wage. Wearing dress likes adult little boys and girls go to field during plantation and harvest and demand full wage from the saukar.

"No breast...No beard... Why Rs. 10/-? Vulgarity often gives good entertainment to working class people and they do hard labour with double vigour. The cunning saukars know very well that these little boys and girls give output of Rs. 7/- with Rs. 5/- half wage whereas adults give Rs. 6/- output hardly working for 3-4 hours a day chitchatting making tall talks. Taking more time and enhancing production cost. Hence through backdoor means they give Rs. 1/- 2/- more to these child labourers and employ them regularly in the field. Thus illiterate needy parents first in agriculture sector in India encouraged child labour.

Little girls used to nurse babies of well-to-do families, clean floor, utensils etc., and employed for indoor menial jobs with negligible wages. Considerate masters sometimes provide left out food, torn clothes and try to please her so that she can continue to work in his house till her marriage.

Later greedy parents sent their children to nearby towns where they were employed in hotels to do odd jobs like plate cleaning, bringing water etc. in automobile garages, child labourer was employed at low wage to do hard works beyond the capacity of their age. They used to torture these children. Play sex with minor girls and these unfortunate creatures used to tolerate all exploitation without any complaint. What to do? Apart from arranging their own food, they had to look after their old ailing dependent parents at home.

Thus a child forgoing all charms of divine childhood worked like a slave with a ruddy merciless master. Is this not a social evil? Why history remained silent all these days till 10.12.1948. When the Human Rights Commission was formed in the global level?

Why the earlier generation never bothered to feel that all human beings from birth till death should have the right of food, education and employment?

This is really an unfortunate state of affair for which every developing country in this world is responsible. International Labour Organization, UNICEF surveyed that there are still 244-million child labour *i.e.* 2.5% of world population. These child labourers are illiterate and poor having dark future. Orissa is 3rd in India as regards child labour. Labour restriction imposed our child labour are violated often and I.L.O pressure to fine the offenders will slowly in prose the world situation. U.N.O provides funds to all countries for rehabilitation of this child labour. Trade training centers with free hostel facility are being opened to educate these labourers and given them self-employment in any trade.

In India 50% of the population are still illiterate. Coming under the poverty lines having annual income of Rs. 8-10,000/- *i.e.* Rs. 30/- per day. Subsidized ration & other essential commodities are being supplied to people, below poverty line. BPL cards are issued to them for getting other benefits. Old age pension is introduced for those who are old and obsolete. Thus better condition is expected if plans and programmes are carried out sincerely with corruption free.

CONCLUSION

Just like child labour, now the organizations in International level should tackle the problems of educated youth unemployment. These young men hate to labour and without any earning. They have become parasites to parental resources. Once that is exhausted they are sure to go to roadway ward and become serious burden to society. Idle mind is devils' workshop and who knows; this devil will come out one day as a "Terrorist". Prevention is always better than cure. World organizations can easily take up this crisis and once these educated youth are given proper employment and source of living. Terrorism will automatically vanish. Then the global slogan for peace will be :

"Work is God, Labour is divine workship it; Man is there to help a man, who needs it."

13

Child Labour : An Indian Perspective

*—Dr. Basant Kumar Behera**

The problem of Child labourers over the years has assumed international dimension. This phenomenon is prevalent through out India cutting across different sectors of the economy. According to an estimate, Child labourers in India number from 44 to 100 million with a bulk of proportion spread over the rural India (2000 A.D). The magnitude of child labour in India has defied all attempts at reaching a solution.

There are a constellation of factors responsible for the constant rise of child labourers in India, such as poverty, economic backwardness, population growth, dispossession of the poor from their lands, defective educational system, insecurity familial problems, unemployment problems etc. These problems are deep rooted in Indian society. A number of social factors are responsible for the health hazards. They are, *inter alia*, poor economic, educational, housing, hygienic and working conditions.

Child labour assumes inhuman form when it degerates and takes the form of slavery, prostitution, debt, bonded and employment in hazardous enterprises. According to an estimate conducted by International Labour Organisation (ILO), one third of 250 millions child labourers do work in hazardous condition. A large chunk of these poverty ridden children reside in South Asian Countries.

In India such children are groaning under slavery or forced labour systems. The systems of debt bondage plays havoc

*Reader and Head, Dept. of History, Digapahandi College, Orissa.

with the lives of the children where they work to meet the obligation of their family. Children spend much of their time in such environments as they grow up so much so that they hardly understand the difference between help rendered to their parents and child labour. Bulk of child labourers hail from poor socio-economic background. Unable to provide two square meals a day to many of their children, parents, under forced circumstances beyond their control, send their children to work as labourers with the hope of alleviating poverty and help the family to eke out a living.

Ihsan Dogramaci in his book published in 1985 on the subject "CHILD LABOUR AND HEALTH" has vividly described the repercussion child labour would have on the impressionable age on the mental and physical growth of children. Children suffers from long hours of strenuous work as their body and mind are not suited to such ventures. Driven by conditions of mainutrition and undernutrition, their power of immunity is lowered thus falling a pray to many diseases. Such labour tell upon the health of the children and soon they fall victims to anemia, malnutrition, fatigue sleeplessness tuberculosis and other infectious diseases.

The phenomenon of child labour and all the problems associated with it, are prevelent in developing countries like India. In India the conditions in which children are given to work, cripples, the child physically mentally and emotionally.

Some times children are made to work in such environment where they come in contact with harmful substances such'as, fire work, industries, match, lock chemicals and baloons or in glass industry or power loom industries where cotton dust cause irreparable damage to the lungs.

India is wedded to a democratic system of governance. Here labour laws are made banning children under fourteen years of age from working in any concern according to the provisions of the Factories Act, Under Factories Act (63 of 1948) section 70, and Article 24 of Indian Constitution, children are prohibited from working at night. Inspite of such provisions children continue to work at night. Sometimes young children between age of seven and eight are allowed to work under unsuitable conditions. Thus labour laws are blatently violated without any fear of punishments by all and sundry.

In defence of continuance of night shift for children, the industrialists argue that cost of production would increase, for the industries would have to employ men instead. Labour department takes a cursory interest in it by dismissing the fact that child labour continues to exist so long as poverty and socio-economic inequalities prevail in the society. The argument could be still stretched to say that certain occupation are heridatory and children should work early to carry forward the ancient art and save it from extinction. Such contention, however, should be summarily rejected in keeping with the provisions of labour laws. With a view to deal with cases of child labour, the child labour laws be amended until child labour is banished from this society look, stock and barrel.

Indian society is stratified between rich and poor, the "haves and have nots." Attempts should be made from all classes of people to correct the loopholes and remove the inherent wicknesses of the society which perpetuates this social malady in the form of child labour.

Steps need to be taken to (1) open special schools for children coming from socio-economically poor sections of the society. (2) Measures may be adopted to bring in socio-economic development of the families reeling under poverty. It should be remembered that solution to the problem of child labour lies in improving the socio-economic profile of the society for which conscious efforts should be made to launch long term plans. Such plans should involve not only Government departments and public institutions but also the community for whom it was conceived and implemented.

Until and unless the political leadership and bureaucracy muster political will and courage to achieve agricultural development, remove rural poverty, unemployment, achieve "FOOD FOR ALL", health care "EDUCATION FOR ALL CHILDREN", children in India will not be able to enjoy a happy childhood and lead a life free from hunger and child labour. In other words if all shades of opinion and all sections of people in this vast countries of ours would address to solve a single problem poverty—which has defied solution so far, the problem of child labour would be solved.

REFERENCES

1. Ihsan Dogramaci, "CHILD LABOUR AND HEALTH", Defence of children international (1985).
2. Indian Constitution Article : 24.
3. Factories Act (63 of 1948) under section 70.
4. Labour Committee Report, April 1986.
5. Child Labour (Prohibition and Regulation) Act, 1986.
6. Amnesty International (1995), "THE CHILDHOOD STOLEN" (London).
7. Hammarberg T. (1989), "THE U.N. CONVENTION ON RIGHTS of CHILD and HOW TO MAKE IT WORK" in special issue of Human Rights Quarterly, Vol. 12.
8. Van, Bueren G. (1995), The International Law on the Rights of the Child, "Save the Children", Martinus Nijhoft, Netherlands.
9. Verhellen E. (ed) (1996), Monitoring children's rights, Martinus Nijhoft, Netherlands.
10. Gandhi, P.R. (1995), International Human Rights, Documents, Blackstone, London.

14

Primary Education and Elimination of Child Labour in India

*—Dr. S.N. Tripathy**

*—Prof. Debadutta Choudhury***

The problem of child labour has drawn the attention of planners, labour administrators, researchers at the global and national level especially after the celebration of International year of the Child 1979.

Estimates of child labour in India, their magnitude by various organisations have been presented in table 14.1. The data postray that though not there is uniformity in the estimation of the volume and magnitude of the problem but positively it is a serious problem in India.

Dr. Tripathy (1991)[1] highlights the employment of children is extensive in agriculture, construction projects, bidi making, Kendu leaf collection, bamboo forest operations and alike. Decline in forest area due to Podu or shifting cultivation, restrictions imposed by the Government in the use of the forests by the tribal people, large-scale transfer of land to the non-tribals, uncertain rainfall and frequent failure of crops—all these entangle the tribals in the web of misery, leading to dropouts of children at the primary school level.

The child labour survey of labour department of Orissa in 1997, complying with supreme court verdict on child labour

*Dr. Tripathy, Department of Economics, Aska Science College.

**Prof. Choudhury is Head, Department of Economics, Samantiapalli College, (Ganjam).

Table 14.1. Estimates of Child Labour in India

Organisation	*Year*	*Magnitude*
1. 1981 Census of India	1981	13.60
2. Human Rights Watch	1981	18.50
3. NSS	1983	17.40
4. Planning commission	1983	17.36
5. Operation Research Group (Baroda)	1983	44.00
6. Labour Ministry	1991	44.00
7. Commission on Labour Standards & International Trade, Government of India	1995	77.00
8. Campaign Against Child Labour	1996	75.00
9. UNICEF*	1996	85.00
10. The Balai Pate Bank, Manila	—	111.00

*Based on Non-School going children and families living in destitution.

in December, 1996 shows two interesting results. First, girl child labourers working in hazardous sectors are more in number (5.6 percent) than their counterparts. Those districts (mostly south west districts) which have low women literacy rates, have high child labour incidence. South West Orissa constitute 57 percent of total identified child labour. Beedi making, brick making, rice mills, stone crushing, blacksmiths etc. absorb an overwhelming 66 percent of total child labour under hazardous occupations. The district Sambalpur has the highest number of boys (1248) child labour and girls (3513) child labour among all the districts under hazardous occupations mostly in beedi making and rice mills. Orissa labour director remarks wisely that about 74 percent of total child labour are compelled to work due to object poverty. Big sized family, parent's inability to afford education cost, death and accidents of parents, ill-habited father etc. and other causes which force the children to work rather than go for education.

Moreover, about 45 to 50 thousand children migrate annually to other parts of the states and even outside the state

Table 14.2. Incidence of Child Labour by Sub-Sectors (1991), 5-14 years age group (%) All.

Sectors	*Boys*	*Girls*
1. Cultivators	37.9	30.8
2. Agricultural Labourers	39.6	51.9
3. Manufacturing in Household Industries	20.4	12.7
4. Others	2.1	4.6

Source : Census of India, 1991.

Table 14.3. Activity Status of Children 5-14 Age Group NCAER Data

States	*Currently enrolled*	*Reported working*	*No where children (Not working & not enrolled)*	*All children*
1. Andhra Pradesh	68.7	9.0	22.3	100.00
2. Assam	68.7	2.6	28.8	100.00
3. Bihar	51.8	3.9	44.3	100.00
4. Gujarat	67.8	6.2	25.9	100.00
5. Haryana	69.0	1.9	29.1	100.00
6. Himachal Pradesh	86.8	0.8	12.4	100.00
7. Karnataka	67.0	7.4	25.6	100.00
8. Kerala	91.1	0.4	8.5	100.00
9. Maharashtra	73.7	8.0	18.3	100.00
10. Madhya Pradesh	52.1	3.5	44.4	100.00
11. Orissa	60.0	5.1	34.6	100.00
12. Punjab	78.7	3.4	17.8	100.00
13. Rajasthan	54.8	1.2	44.0	100.00
14. Tamilnadu	73.0	5.6	21.3	100.00
15. Uttar Pradesh	56.7	1.5	41.8	100.00
16. West Bengal	57.1	6.7	36.2	100.00
All States	61.9	4.3	33.8	100.00

Source : Duraisamy, M. (2000), Child Schooling and Child Work in India, Paper Written for NCAER, New Delhi, under its "Programme of Research in Human Development".

as bonded child labour. Mainly, such child labourers are migrated from the tribal dominated blocks of Koraput, Malkangiri, Nawarangpur, Keonjhar, Kalahandi, Bolangir and Sundergarh districts of Orissa. It has been observed that, in addition to the bonded child labour, there are child labourers originated from the coastal districts of Ganjam and Puri who work in textile, handlooms of Surat (Gujarat) estimating more than one lakhs (below 15 years).

It is obvious from the table 14.2 that most of the child labourers are employed in agricultural sector in India as per census of 1991. Compared to males, female child labourers are proportionately at a higher rate in agricultural sector.

Table 14.3, presents the activity status of children in the age group of 5-14 years collected through National Council of Applied Economic Research (NCAER). The data reveals that in Andhra Pradesh the highest percentage of children have been reported working followed by Karnataka. Madhya Pradesh, Bihar, Rajasthan and Uttar Pradesh states represent the maximum percentage of no-where children—the percentage being 44.4, 44.3, 44.0 and 41.8 respectively. In all India level the percentage of no-where children (not working and nor enrolled) is 33.8 as revealed from the table.

The 52nd Round of NSS shows that there are about 230.8 million children in the age group 6-14 yrs. in 1995-96. About 61 percent of these children were attending school which indicates that 39 percent estimating 90 million children in the said age group were out of schools in 1995-96.

Table 14.4 depicts the data relating to reason for non-enrollment of children in the age of group of 5-14 during the year 1995-96. It is revealed from the table that lack of interest in studies is the important factor for non-enrollment of children in India. The other vital reason is 'direct economic factors'.

Table 14.5, reflects the gender-wise drop-out rates at primary and upper primary stages in India. It is demonstrated from the table that during the period 1980-81 to 1995-96, there has been a declining trend of dropout rates in India. At primary

Table 14.4. Research for Non-Enrollment of Children (Age Group 5-14) Percentage 1995-96

Reason for 'Never Enrollment' Household Expenditure

	Classes					
All children	*Bottom*	*2nd*	*3rd*	*4th*	*Top*	*All*
Lack of interest in studies	48.6	48.5	52.0	47.8	48.7	49.1
Direct school related factors	4.7	3.9	4.3	4.9	7.0	4.7
Direct economic actors	27.2	25.3	22.3	21.0	16.0	24.0
Others	19.5	22.3	21.4	26.3	28.3	22.2
Total	100.00	100.00	100.00	100.00	100.00	100.00
Rural Girls						
Lack of interest in studies	49.3	49.7	53.9	48.8	54.0	50.7
Direct school related factors	5.8	4.5	4.3	5.1	7.0	5.2
Direct economic factors	26.0	24.6	21.4	20.6	15.6	23.1
Others	18.4	21.2	20.2	25.5	23.4	21.0
Total	100.00	100.00	100.00	100.00	100.00	100.00

Source : Tilak, J.B.G. (2000), "Education Poverty in India", National Institute of Educational Planning & Administration, Occasional paper 29, New Delhi.

stage, the dropout rate was 56.20 among boys in 1980-81 which decreased to 37.79 during 1995-96. Among the Girls the percentage has been declined from 62.5% to 37.92% during the said period.

In the upper primary stage, the percentage of dropouts during 1980-81 was 68% which declined to 54.99 in 1995-96. Among the girls the percentage of dropout was 79.4% in 1980-81 which decreased to 61.7% in 1995-96.

However, despite falling trend of dropouts, the percentage

Table 14.5. Gender-Wise Dropout Rates at Primary and Upper Primary Stages in India

(In Percentage)

Year	*Primary Stage*		*Upper primary stage*	
	Boys	*Girls*	*Boys*	*Girls*
1980-81*	56.20	62.50	68.00	79.40
1984-85*	45.62	51.41	61.83	70.87
1989-90*	46.35	50.35	61.00	68.75
1995-96**	37.79	37.92	54.99	61.70

Source : *Women in India : A statistical Profile (1997), Department of Women & Child Development, Government of India, New Delhi, PP.90-91.

**Statistics on children in India, Packet Book (1997), New Delhi, p. 190.

is still higher among girls? compared to girls in India both at Primary as well as Upper Primary levels. Hence, in the context of new economic policy, globalisation and liberalisation, it is pertinent to focus the problem of child labour.

Besides, liberalisation has been accompanied by a concerted mode to cut welfare schemes which benefit the poor. One example of this is the cut-back in budget for Primary education, which will deny a huge mass of Indian children the right to basic education. The withdrawal of the mid-day meal scheme is another indication of a thatcherite mentality which seems to have gripped an influential section of decision makers. While farmers especially the rich, are being wooed in Maharashtra, Punjab and other states with subsidies, interest, free loans, non-payment of out-standing debts and abolition of power tariff, which in turn leads to huge losses for the public exchequer, poor children are being deprived of the maximum 100 grams of calories the magic potion of cheap rice and a thin curry to cope with hunger.

Cases of children falling ill after consuming meals provided by the Government, the massive corruption and siphoning at food stock, have become common in many parts of the country. All this is unpondorable where there are more than 320 million people below the poverty line, a majority of whom are perennial mal-nourished, or starving.

States have, over the years exhibited utter lack of discipline in financial management, especially when it concerns the social sector-core areas like health, nutrition, education, family planning and employment.

Though the number of schools had gone up, there are several regional, gender and caste factors which contributed to high dropout rates at the primary stage itself. Moreover, growing pauperisation among the masses is making more and more children vulnerable to exploitation.

According to the UNICEF's report on 'The State of the World's Children-1997' (which focused on child labour), "The most powerful force driving children into hazardous habilitating labour is the exploitation of poverty. Where society is characterised by poverty and irregularity, the incidence of child labour is likely to increase, as does the risk that it is exploitative. The parents of child labourers are often unemployed or employed, desperate for secure employment and income." Ironically, it is not they, but their children, who are offered hobs—obviously because the younger the workers the simpler it is to exploit them."

The vital links between economic hardship and child labour were also confirmed by studies conducted by a number of Non-Governmental Organisations for the department of Women and Child Development, Government of Karnataka, in 1995.

For instance, in one study, more than 90 percent of the child workers covered mentioned the financial circumstances of the family and parental debt as the main reason for their situation. Two studies revealed that the parents of child labourers are overwhelmingly employed in the unorganised sector of labour. Of those working in this highly exploitative sector, where there is no assurance of even statutory minimum wages more than two thirds were found to be causal labourers, who do not know from day-to-day whether they will get any work at all.

Clearly this situation must be effectively addressed if the children of these families—who make up a large proportion of the country's population—are to avoid the pitful of child labour.

Yet another study made the point that income from working children is often the sole factor that enables economically disadvantaged families to float above the poverty line. According to the researchers, when the financial contribution of these children is deducted from the family income, many more families slip under the poverty line and ignoring the debilitating deprivation suffered by the majority of the population will surely not help alter this harsh reality.

In fact, poverty cannot be seen solely in monetary terms. Although economic deprivation is possibly the most visible aspect of poverty, several social, cultural, political and even geographical factors contribute to the experience of poverty, in turn, to child labour. For instance, children are often forced to work because the poor have little or no access to basic needs not just because of inadequate income but because of various socio-cultural and political factors (among them caste, community and gender), which deny or restrict their access to resources and opportunities, including survival needs and fundamental human rights.

As a 1995 "save the children" publication entitled "Towards a children's Agenda; New challenges for social Development", put it, poverty is the "inability to participate fully in the life of society—economically, politically, socially and culturally." A nation which claims to be democratic cannot afford to have the majority of its population, including its children, thus disabled.

The UNICEF report points out "Poverty begets child labour begets lack of education begets poverty".

In other words, while poverty creates the conditions for child labour, child labour clearly condemns working children to a life of unskilled work and ignorance, which further ensnares them in continuing poverty and illiteracy.

The OSLO Meeting, jointly organised by the Government of Norway, UNICEF and the International Labour Organisation (ILO), recognised that while strategies for poverty reduction and elimination need to address the problem of child labour, the interconnection between child labour and the social conditions of the child and his/her family must be at the center of sustainable social development policies. The UNICEF report also acknowledges and validates both sides of the education-child labour argument (one insisting that the strict enforcement of compulsory education alone will solve the problem and the other questioning the very worth of the present education system). While lack of access to relevant education is one of the root causes of child labour, it says, "Education has become part of the problem. It has to be reborn as part of the solution."

Similarly, while accepting the fact that "education, particularly basic education, is one of the principal means of preventing and eliminating child labour, the OSLO document goes on to stress the importance of establishing a system of accessibility, relevant, high quality, universal, and compulsory basic education that is free for all". In India, which has a large network of private institutions catering to the needs of the affluent, public resources must clearly be used primarily to expand, modify and upgrade the public educational system so that it is actually free and accessible, as well as relevant, enjoyable and good quality. For this the Government's investment in primary, if not elementary education must be stepped up and, equally importantly, put to effective use.

In India, child labour is keeping children out of school, thereby contributing to the growth of illiteracy. Employers in industries compact with schools for the children, that too with government support. Children are generally recruited by brokars belonging to their own villages. These middlemen are paid commission or their services.

Today, it is part of official policy the world-over that children should not be kept out of school no matter how poor their parents are. Unfortunately, in India, neither is primary education compulsory nor child labour illegal, Indian law prohibits employment of children in factories but not in cottage industries, households, restaurants or in agriculture.

Given the absence of stricter child labour laws or any provision for compulsory education, approximately more than 82.2 million children in India between the ages six and fourteen years do not go to school.

Unfortunately, no worthwhile campaign has been launched to successfully appeal to the conscience of the authorities or the Indian Public. The popular refrain that poor parents should not be forced to send their children to school is more politically motivated than concerned with social justice. Implementation of effective child labour laws would go against the interests of powerful employers. There is, therefore, a negative element forwarded as both the moral and practical reason for the prevalence of child labour.

Children come to acquire skills through employment and not education. They are a preferred workforce for they are more pliable than adults, work for lower wages and are not unionised. The irony here is that since independence, every government at the centre, all Government-appointed commissions and all opposition parties have advocated the abolition of child labour. They have pretended to uphold the cause of compulsory universal and primary education to all children upto the age of 14 years.

WESTERN VIEWS TOWARDS INDIA'S "BELIEF SYSTEM"

The west—be it in the form of its political leaders, academics of social activities—do not accept India's low per capita income and economic situation alone cause its child labour problem. It blames the "belief system" shared by the bureaucracy, many educators and social activists and by broad sections of the middle class.

At the care of this system is the Indian view of the social order including the respective roles of the upper and lower classes. Literacy is a means to maintain social disparities given that "excessive or inappropriate education for the poor and disrupt existing social arrangements".

As a result, the governing elites—which otherwise profess to be socialists—believe in reinforcing rather than destroying the divide between "people who work with their minds and people who work with their hands and are ruled". According to the west, the caste system is responsible for this mindset. Values related to status are thought too deeply imbedded in Indian culture.

Secondly, contrary to popular belief, it is difficult to establish a relationship between literacy and per capita income. What India spends of its gross national product on education is less than what other nations do. Moreover, a large part of India's education budget goes to higher education.

Policy makers dealing with child labour overlook two vital points. First, though the poor welcome the benefits accruing from child labour, a large number of adults are displaced from the labour market. Second, families are provided with a few family planning incentives.

Indian Government gave into international pressure by deciding to phase out children hazardously employed in carpet weaving, stone quarrying, wool cleaning and match and fire works industries. But to take care of the child labourers and to reduce their number, school retention rates will have to be increased.

REFERENCES

1. Tripathy, S.N., Exploitation of Child Labour in Tribal India, Daya Publishing House, Delhi, 1991.
2. Tripathy, S.N. & Das, C.R., Migrant labour in India, Discovering Publishing House, New Delhi, 1997.
3. Tilak, J.B.G., Educational Poverty in India, National Institute of Educational, Planning and Administration, Occasional paper 29, New Delhi, 2000.

15

Issues and Problems of Child Labour in India

—*Dr. M. Mishra**

INTRODUCTION

An important issue in human resources development is prevalence of child labour. At present child labour remains one of the most evocative and controversial challenges of the world. The working child representative of all unjust and exploitations of industrialization is still with us even in the most advanced societies of the world. The inexorable linkages of child labour with poverty, education, health and gender highlight the need for broad-based social and economic progress. The sheer size and ramifications of the child working population in many poorer countries has spurred extensive review and policy initiatives (Fallon and Tzannatos 1998, UNICEF 1997, US Department Labour 1994, 1995, 1996). The 1997 *State of the World's Children* (UNICEF 1997) focused on hazardous and exploitative child labour, and described barriers to as well as opportunities for reducing the negative impact of child labour. International legal positions have been extensively reviewed, as has progress toward the ratification of various treaties for the protection of children (Fallon and Tzannatos 1998, Interanational Conference on Child Labour 1997). The International Labour Organization (ILO) has an active portfolio of activities in this arena and a specific

*Lecturer in Economics, Science College, Hinjilicut-761102, Ganjam, Orissa, India.

programme, the international Programme for the Elimination of Child Labour (IPEC) that focuses on data collection and programmes for the elimination of hazardous child labour (Forastieri, 1997). Child labour though widely prevalent in the poor developing countries of the world it is universal in nature and is found everywhere irrespective of its level of socioeconomic development (Madhok, 1996). The 1997 *State of the World's Children* (UNICEF 1997) states even in highly developed countries there exists the menace of child labour. In the countries like United Kingdom 11 year old children constitute between 15 to 26% and 15-year-old children constitute between 33 to 66% of child labour in its work force. Equally true is the situation in United States because it recorded a 250% rise in child labour during 1983-1990 (Pattanaik and Bedi, 1998). Though the problem is global in nature, it has assumed serious dimensions in the developing countries like India.

WHAT IS CHILD LABOUR

Child labour is generally regarded as the employment of children less than 18 years of age (Landrigan *et al.*, 1998). If possible, age categories must be further stratified, since the health and educational implications of work for a 17-year-old differ substantially from those for a 10-year-old. Not all working children are paid for their work; many are doing "domestic work" or in bonded labour, unpaid "apprenticeships" or as slaves. There is no consistently reliable, updated source of data on child labour. Most reports rely on anecdotal evidence or limited cross-sectional studies (US Department of Labour 1995; International Conference on Child Labour 1997).

The term 'Child Labour' at times, used as a synonym for 'employed child' or 'working child'. In this sense it is co-extensive with any work done by a children for gain. But Dr. V.V. Giri has interpreted child labour in two different senses, first as an economic practice and secondly as a social evil. The child labour, therefore, in restricted sense means the employment of children in gainful occupations, which are harmful for their health and deny them opportunity to grow (Mahapatra, 1997). According to the Human Development Report of the UNDP, child labour is not an economic necessity of poor parents; rather it is the consequence of extreme social and economic exploitation. The United Nations defines child labour as any work that hampers child's eduction, tortures his/her psyche and does not allow him to enjoy social and moral development. All work done by a child is not labour, but the labour that exploits him/her is called child labour (Pattanaik and Bedi, 1998).

Child labour has not generally accepted definitions but a widely accepted definition connotes that child below 15 years of age working voluntarily or under compulsion in organized or unorganized sectors to earn a livelihood for themselves or for their family. According to ILO "Child Labour includes children permanently leading adult lives, working long hours for low wages under conditions damaging to their health and to their physical and mental development, sometimes separated from their families, frequently deprived of meaningful educational and training opportunities that could open up for them a better future.

WHAT LEADS TO CHILD LABOUR

The basic cause of child labour is poverty of the family (Sinha, 2000). Abject poverty is the main cause of child labour throughout the world. Poor parents treat children as economic asset and send them to work at an early age to ameliorate the poverty of the family. Young children seek employment very early because augmentation of their income is highly essential for the survival of the invariably large families, illiteracy ignorance, low wage rate, unemployment, social prejudices, backwardness and poor standard of living are mainly responsible for the causes of child labour in poor countries like India (Madhok, 1996). Also a fast growing population, migration to urban areas, family disintegration, inadequate social security provisions, defective institutional arrangements and ineffective legal machinery contribute a lot to this problem. The mounting number of educated unemployed youth undermines the faith on the efficacy of education, leads to more drop-outs and increasing child labour (Anandharajkumar, 1999). The low wage structure of the adult workman also has a direct bearing on the extent of child labour.

Apart from this the other economic causes are also important for the creation of child labour. Children work in all the sectors and work at a low wage rate for a longer duration of hours work. Further, since they are flexible both mentally and physically, they are moulded easily to the exploitative tactics of the employers. Their inability to protest along with poor implementation of child labour laws leads to further increase in the number of child labour. To summarise, child labour exists due to low socio-economic status of poor parents on the one hand and the commercial and profiteering interests of the employers on the other. The existence of child labour, therefore, is not due to poverty alone, it is the exploitation of that poverty in a profitable manner (Pattanaik and Bedi, 1998).

Domestic labour for young girls is the most common form of employment in the developing countries of Asia, more particularly in India (Madhok, 1996). But it is surprising that no proper data is available to this effect and due recognition is not accorded to the working girl child labour (Saisab, 1998). Various studies reveal that Indian girl child are employed in many common household works like fetching of water, collection of fuel wood, looking after young children, rearing cattle and many more which are not recognized as child labour and this perhaps is due to the socio-cultural belief of the Indian society. The neglect of woman child labour is due to many causes, but in a male dominated society with deliberate neglect to female child undermines their status. However, such gender-biased discrimination is not just. The issues of child labour cannot be viewed properly without appreciating the problem of girl child labour, which constitutes a large number.

Illiteracy, ignorance, low wage rate, unemployment, social prejudices, backwardness and poor standard of living are mainly responsible for the causes of child labour in poor countries like India (Madhok, 1996). Also a fast growing population, migration to urban areas, family disintegration, inadequate social security provisions, defective institutional arrangements and ineffective legal machinery contribute a lot to this problem. The mounting number of educated unemployed youth undermines the faith on the efficacy of education, leads to more drop-outs and increasing child labour (Anandharajkumar, 1999). The low wage structure of the adult workman also has a direct bearing on the extent of child labour.

Apart from this the other economic causes are also important for the creation of child labour. Children work in all the sectors and work at a low wage rate for a longer duration of hours work. Further, since they are flexible both mentally and physically, they are moulded easily to the exploitative tactics of the employers. Their inability to protest along with poor implementation of child labour laws leads to further increase in the number of child labour. To summarise, child labour exists due to low socio-economic status of poor parents on the one hand and the commercial and profiteering interests of the employers on the other. The existence of child labour, therefore, is not due to poverty alone, it is the exploitation of that poverty in a profitable manner (Pattanaik and Bedi, 1998).

Domestic labour for young girls is the most common form of employment in the developing countries of Asia, more particularly in India (Madhok, 1996). But it is surprising that no proper data is available to this effect and due recognition is not accorded to the working girl child labour (Saisab, 1998). Various studies reveal that Indian girl child are employed in many common household works like fetching of water, collection of fuel wood, looking after young children, rearing cattle and many more which are not recognized as child labour and this perhaps is due to the socio-cultural belief of the Indian society. The neglect of woman child labour is due to many causes, but in a male dominated society with deliberate neglect to female child undermines their status. However, such gender-biased discrimination is not just. The issues of child labour cannot be viewed properly without appreciating the problem of girl child labour, which constitutes a large number.

MAGNITUDE OF CHILD LABOUR

Child labour contributes significantly to the Indian economy as 20% of the GNP comes from the contributions of child labour and child workers constitute 8% of the total work force. Most of the export industries like carpets, textiles, diamond etc. in India are based on child labour and low wage paid to them perhaps the best comparative advantage of engaging child labour in gainful employment. The social scenario according to the Gurupadswami Committee on child labour changed radically with the advent of industrialization and urbanization. The recent industrial development and the era of globalisation induced the use of child labour in the profit making export activities. In the recent years there occurred a drastic change in the nature of child work as they moved out of their families to the distant places being engaged in hazardous occupations instead of being a part of agricultural and artisanal labour within the families with enjoyment of leisure and play.

Child labour may be more prevalent in developing countries but it is definitely a universal problem. As per the latest ILO report, the number of child labour in the world has reached an outstanding figure of 250 millions. At least 120 million children in developing countries work full-time and another 130 millions part-time (Forastieri, 1997). According to the ILO, 125 millions work in hazardous industries. Of the total 250 millions, 177 millions come from six developing countries. A continental distribution narrates that Asia has 153, Africa 80 and Latin America 17 millions respectively. In Africa, about 40% of all children between 5 and 14 are engaged in childhood earnings in doing some work. In fact, in most countries with a Gross Domestic Product (GDP) per capita of $500 and less, economically active children comprise a significant proportion of the total labour force. In these countries, between 30-60% of the children are in the labour force (Lemen *et al.* 1993; Fallon and Tzannatos, 1998). Child labour is not confined to less-developed countries. Economic transition brings with it shifts in the prevalence and nature of child labour. Even in the former socialist economies also it is observed that the nature and extent of child labour is increasing in number. In Spain more than hundred thousand children work in orchards and plantations. The USA has seen a resurgence of child labour due to a range of factors. These include household poverty levels, changes in labour market demographics, the availability of low-skilled jobs in the service sector, and a relaxation of regulation, inspection and enforcement of child labour laws (Postol, 1993; Landrigan, 1993; Landrigan *et al.* 1995; Academy of Pediatrics, 1995; Landrigan, *et al.* 1998). Farm workers union reported in 1985 that millions of young hands are employed in farms and plantation. The ILO study in the department of Marde de Dios has revealed that 20 per cent of the workers deployed in gold production are between the 11-18 years of age. Thousands of children in the western world work in fast food joints, gas stations, sells news papers, clean cars and work in garment and leather factories (Madhok, 1996).

Of the total world child labour India, Pakistan and Bangladesh constitute the highest number. In India 37% of people are below the poverty line who compels their children to earn a livelihood very early (Pattanaik and Bedi, 1998). So regarding child labour India tops the list among the South Asian neighbours. Though authentic statistics is not available, yet India probably has the highest number about 25 per cent of working children in the world. Different estimates regarding the population of child labour do not offer a uniform picture. According to ILO statistics, India perhaps has the largest child labour. Approximately 45 million children are employed in both organized and unorganized sectors, working for an average of 10 to 12 hours daily for a very low wage of Rs. 250 per month (Anandharajkumar, 1999). As per 1991 census the worker-population ratio for the age group between 05-15 comes to 5.4%. As per the study Andhra Pradesh has highest number of child labour, 1.66 millions. Among the districts, Jhabua in Madhya Pradesh has the highest 17% and Lakshadweep the lowest 0.13%. Incidentally, the districts where child labour was highest also had a poor record of literacy, particularly female literacy. Over 90 per cent of child labour are concentrated in rural areas of eleven states. (Table

15.1). Though child labour is found in all states of India irrespective of the nature of the economy, whether agriculture or industry and rural and urban, concentration of child workers is more prominent in the states like Andhra Pradesh, Madhya Pradesh, Rajasthan, Orissa, Bihar, Karnataka, Maharasthra and Tamilnadu. In Orissa 60% of labour force is below the age of 14 years. A state wise distribution says Andhra Pradesh ranks first in the country.

Orissa accounts for 6% of the total child labour against its share of around 5% of the total child population. As per the Labour Statistics of Orissa (1997) there are 2.15 lakhs children employed (56.50% male and 43.50% female) in various work establishments and of them 0.24 lakhs engaged in hazardous occupation. A spatial overview reveals greater child work participation in the tribal districts of Orissa. Kalahandi tops the list with 11.30% whereas the economically advanced

Table 15.1. Statewise Distribution of Child Labour in India

States	*Main workers*	*Marginal workers*	*Total workers*	*Percentage of child workers to total*	
				Popula-tion	*Workers*
Andhra Pradesh	1537293	124647	1661940	2.50	5.53
Bihar	759444	146801	942245	1.09	3.35
Gujarat	373027	150558	523585	1.26	3.07
Karnataka	818159	158088	976247	2.16	3.07
Madhya Pradesh	997940	354623	1352583	2.04	5.16
Maharashtra	805847	262571	1068418	1.35	3.16
Orissa	325250	127144	452394	1.42	3.80
Rajasthan	490522	283677	774199	1.76	4.57
Tamilnadu	523125	55764	578889	1.03	2.34
Uttar Pradesh	1145087	264999	1410086	1.01	3.14
West Bengal	593387	118304	711691	1.04	3.23

Source : Pattanaik and Bedi (1998).

districts like Cuttack is ranked the lowest only with 2.61% of child work participation. A sectorial distribution of child labour indicates higher concentration in the primary sector (88.16%) while the secondary and tertiary sectors account for 4.25 and 7.59 per cent respectively. The important economic activities of child labour in Orissa include fishing, shrimp farming, non-timber forest products, bidi manufacturing, rice mills, tobacco industry, stone cutting and polishing, hotels and garages, majority of which are hazardous in nature. It is also noticed that on account of increasing restrictions more and more of child labour concentrated in the unorganized sector. Employment of child labour is higher in rural sector than the urban in Orissa. In the rural there are 75.4% male and 24.6% female where as in the urban there are 73% of male and 27% of female child workers.

DIMENSIONS OF CHILD LABOUR

1. *Concentrated in Rural Areas :* Various estimates made by the Census of India, NSS and NCAER favour that child labour is more concentrated in the rural areas than in urban centers. From the studies of Census of India and NCAER it is observed that the percentage of child labour in rural areas is even more than two times of the urban areas. Further it is found that it is more in favour of male child than female child though the gap is not significant.
2. *It has been Declining Over Time :* The NSS data over 1977-78 and 1993-94 shows that the incidence of child labour is declining over time in both rural and urban areas.
3. *Concentrated in 10-14 Age Group and in Agriculture :* It is found from recent research that though concentration of child labour is declining over time but it is concentrated in the age group of 10-14 years (14% in rural and 5.6% in urban areas. This also shows a declining trend over time). Further it is observed that child labour concentrates in agricultural labour as it constitutes about 78% for boys and 83% for girls.

4. *Higher Incidence in SCs and STs :* Among the social groups it is found that child labour concentrates more among the Scheduled caste population followed by the scheduled tribes and this is true for both the agricultural as well as non-agricultural labour.
5. *Wide Spread Regional Disparity :* There are significant regional disparities in the distribution of child labour in India. It is very high the southern states like Andhra Pradesh, Tamilnadu and Karnataka and relatively less in the poorer states like Bihar and U.P.

SOCIO-ECONOMIC CONSEQUENCES OF CHILD LABOUR

Child labour is a social evil. According to the World Bank Labour Report 1992, child labour could be considered as 'forced labour' (Madhok, 1996), since children are not in a position to judge and consent the type of work they perform. Many children get bonded earlier to pay family debt and work under appalling conditions (Pattanaik and Bedi, 1998). It stands for economic exploitation, social injustice and degraded cultural and value system. Child labour degenerates the socio-economic structure, affects the social infrastructure, causes health hazards and disturbs the ecology of civil welfare. The huge quantities of child labour have adversely affected the quality of Indian Labour and restricted the scope of adult employment. In rural areas, participation of child labour forces the elder members to migrate. Besides, the prevalence of child labour leads to formation of deliquent groups, anti socials, resulting in human resources underdevelopment (Anandharajkumar, 1999).

Child labour signifies employment of children in several gainful occupations, which are detrimental to their future normal growth and hamper their physical, mental moral and social growth. They are engaged in various hazardous works subject to very harsh working conditions with a unduly longer working hours under adverse working conditions for a very poor remuneration as a result of which nearly fifty per cent of these children never reach the age of twelve, succumbing to malnutrition and diseases.

Social capital an important asset of a nation that promotes harmony and cooperation for mutual benefit is lost due to the practice of child labour as the system lacks basic resources to nurture the most important asset the young. Child labour limits the opportunities of being educated and this has serious socio-economic implications in case of girl child since education determines the child survival and health. Denying education to girls restricts the benefits of reduced fertility and higher family income and it also adversely effects the health of the future generations.

Changes in world economic order that is the liberalization, privatisation and globalisation affect child labour especially in the manufacturing sector. Several corporations, large manufacturing units in which child workers work under unsafe working conditions, hazardous chemicals and poor air quality. Along with this they are remunerated at levels much below than what is required to maintain an adequate standard of living (Cushman, 1998). These human and environment conditions lead to serious health repercussions for the working child.

Modern factory system with advanced technology forces the workers to undertake intense, repetitive tasks which are monotonous in nature for the young children causing repetitive work injuries and deformities. Use of and expose to intensified electrification and machinery also haver serious health implications and loss of welfare. The trade liberalization caused the movement of polluting units from the rich affluent to the poor backward economies. As a result industrial areas have higher levels of pollution and the working children are therefore susceptible to respiratory ailments and long-term health hazards. A World Health Organisation report on the conditions of child labour stated other hazards like bony lesions, postural deformity, weak eyesight, and deformed bone structure in the growing children (Madhok, 1996). Apart from this Violence in the work place is also a common phenomenon that involves heavy health cost.

COMBATING CHILD LABOUR

Child labour as a serious socio-economic problem calls for immediate attention. The government is coming forward with suitable steps to combat child labour. It is making various efforts to monimise the child labour by announcing various programmes and plans.

Constitutional Provisions to Control Child Labour

Article 24 of the Indian Constitution prohibits for the employment of children below 14 years. It says that no children below the age of 14 years shall be employed in any factory or mine or engaged in any other hazardous employment.

Article 39 clause 'e' says that state shall ensure that health and strength of workers, men and women and the tender age of children are not abused and that citizen are not forced by economic necessity to enter evocations unsuited to their age or strength.

Clause 'f' of Article 39 states that children are given opportunities and facilities to develop in a healthy manner and in conditions of freedom and dignity and youth are protected against exploitation and against moral and material abandonment.

Article 45 has the provision that state shall endeavor to provide free and compulsory education for all children until they complete the age of 14 years.

But it is apathetic that instead of the constitutional provisions, child labour continues at a higher scale. The jurists on a Convention on National Public hearing on Child Labour expressed deep concern over the failure of implementation of the Article 45.

Legal Provisions

In India child labour prohibition acts/laws have a long historical background. The laws like Pledging the Children Act, 1937; Employment of Children Act, 1938; Factory Act, 1948; Mines Act, 1952; and Plantation Labour Act, 1957 which deals with the age of entry to employment are famous in this regard. In terms of legislative measures, the most significant effort to tackle child labour is the Child Labour Prohibition and Regulation Act, 1986. Following this act of 1986, the Government adopted the National Child Labour Policy (NCLP), to curb the practice of child labour and initiated several development schemes to rehabilitate them. Under the project based action plan 11 NCLP projects operating in 76 districts with higher concentration of child labour. The project aimed at providing non-formal education, vocational training, supplementary nutrition, stipend and health care. International agencies, NGOs along with the government are associated with the project. The Government of India is making various efforts to minimize the child labour by announcing various plans and programmers.

In 1981, a Central Advisory Board on Child Labour was constituted by the central government to review the plans and schemes, legislations enacted by the government from time to time. The Board was reconstituted in 1994 by incorporating the representatives from the related ministries and departments, members of the parliament, trade union members, NGOs under the chairmanship of the Union Labour Minister. In 1994, the National Authority for the Elimination of Child Labour (NAECL), a high power body was formed with the Chairmanship of the Union Labour Minister to eliminate child labour from hazardous industries, ensure convergence of existing plans and policies, and to coordinate among the child labour related programmes of different related ministries.

In 1994 the government introduced a major programme of special schools in order to withdraw child labour from hazardous occupations. As a follow up of this programme the National Authority for the Elimination of Child Labour was constituted which aimed at the elimination of child labour particularly in the hazardous employment. The Authority aimed at providing health, education and other such services/ inputs to the children taken out of school in a cost effective manner by pooling resources from various ministries.

In December 1996 the Supreme Court of India took a historical step of eliminate child labour. The Supreme Court identified nine hazardous industries and directed for the end of child labour there. For the offenders, the court fixed a fine of Rs. 20,000/- per child labour and alternative employment of adult member of the family. The court also suggested for the formation of Child Labour Rehabilitation-cum-Welfare fund, which may properly look after the health, education, and proper growth of the Child Labour withdrawn.

In July 1997 the State Labour Ministers Conference at New Delhi decided for 100 percent ban on child labour ensuring that no child in the age group of 06-14 years go to work. The conference also emphasized on making right to education as a Fundamental Right as an effective Prohibitory arrangement against child labour.

The Common Minimum Programme (CMP), by the government seeks to eliminate child labour from all occupations and industries making free and compulsory elementary education as a Fundamental Right. The programme states that while Ministry of Labour is responsible for elimination and rehabilitation of child labour, the Department of Education should look after strictly and carefully that the working children get free and compulsory elementary education.

The government of India also drawn up a large number of schemes through its constituent ministries to deal with child labour. Apart from the Ministry of Labour, a few important programmes are coordinated by other ministries as well. The contributions of the Ministry of Human Resources Development and Ministry of Welfare for the upliftment, education, welfare of the street children are noteworthy. The National Policy on Education, 1986 revealed the importance and role of education policy with regard to working children. The NPE stresses the need to continue non formal education, established Non-formal Education centers for the working children, school drop outs and the girls who cannot attend schools. To reach these children, the NPE, 1986 stated a well-defined open learning system.

Policy Issues

1. Economic growth and eradication of poverty : Eradication of poverty, economic growth and improved standard of living certainly would help in reducing child labour. An increase in the adult wage rate is important to reduce the supply of child labour.
2. Beyond poverty-Compulsory education : Provision of compulsory education for the children would necessarily help in reducing child labour. However, compulsory education here should not simply mean the law imbibed arrangements rather it should be a compulsion on the part of the Govt to provide adequate facilities for free education and also it is obligatory on the part of the parental community to send all children to school.
3. Focus on Girl Child : Girl child labour is endowed with certain special problems that need special attention. So educating girl must be the first and foremost priority in attending to their problems. Since education is a prerequisite for their socio-economic independence and a healthy living special arrangements and special investments should be made for their education. An improvement in their educational status will successfully bring them back to the main stream education and control drop outs, which further will help in reducing child labour.
4. Role of NGOs : Government alone is not sufficient in reducing child labour. It is observed in many parts of our country that NGOs been involved in various developmental activity. Their effort for improvement of education is quite useful in eradicating the social evils like child labour. To name a few : Ekalavya in M.P., Lok Jumbish in Rajasthan and MV Foundation in A.P., are actively involved in reducing child labour. It is needed that more of such NGOs should come forward in the states where there is larger concentration of child labour.

CONCLUSIONS

Despite the laws and measures dealing with child labour, the stark reality is that, the impact on child labour has been minimal. It has remained intractably a big problem since long. A closer look at the programmes and policies reveals the very nature of its having no impact on child labour. Simply it is understood that people in the lower economic strata cannot survive unless the children in the family also work. Hence child labour is an inevitable consequence of the economic forces operating on a family. So abolition of child labour without adequate to support to economic status of the families is unthinkable. Legislation would be effective only when child labour become a marginal factor in the process of capitalist accumulation and production. So only those policies would be helpful in reducing child labour that aim at altering modes of production and exploitation. This issue should be dealt in a wider spectrum and broader perspective. Development schemes should be implemented specially for the parents to make the families economically sound. Rights of children must be protected, the silent dehumanization to be averted. Greater amount of public awareness will help a lot to go ahead with the policies.

Children in our country will be able to lead a happy life with some amount of political will to seriously address the issues of agricultural stagnation, rural poverty, unemployment, minimum wages, food security, health care and meaningful education to the millions of labourer families. Morality on the parts of parents and society adds much to this. A self regulatory course by the industries that employ child labour along with removal of poverty only can save the society from this social crime.

REFERENCES

1. Agarwal, A. (1998), "Child Labour in Glass Industry", *Yojana*, Dec., 1998, pp. 21-23.
2. Anandharajkumar (1999), "Child Labour : Issues and Solutions", Kurukshetra, July, 1999, pp. 35-39.

3. Ananthapadmanabhan (1996), "Labouring Lives", The Hindu, Nov., 10, 1996, pp. IV.

4. Cushman, J.H., 1998, Nike pledges to end child labour and apply U.S. rules abroad. The New York Times, May 13 : CI.

5. Dev, S. M. (2000), "Child Labour in India : Dimension, Determinants and Policies', 83rd Annual Conference Volume of the Indian Economic Association, Jammu, 2000, pp. 417-40.

6. Fallon P., Tzannatos Z. (1998), "Child Labour : Issues and directions for the World Bank." Washington DC, The World Bank.

7. Forastieri, V. (1997), "Children at Work : Health and Safety Risks", Geneva : International Labour Office.

8. Graitcer, P.L. and L.B. Lerer (1998), "Child Labour and Health : Quantifying the Global Health Impacts of Child Labour", Washington DC, The World Bank. (Web based).

9. International Conference on Child Labour (1997), "Strategies for eliminating child labour : prevention, removal and rehabilitation—Synthesis document (Oslo, 27-30 October 1997)", Geneva : International Labour Office. New York : United Nations Children's Fund.

10. Landrigan P.J. (1993), "Child Labour : a re-emergent threat", [editorial]. American Journal of Industrial Medicine. 24 : 267-268.

11. Landrigan P.J., Pollack S.H. Belville R. Godbold J.H. (1995), "Child Labour", Pediatric Annals 24 : 657-662.

12. Androgens P.J., Pollack S.H., Belville R., Godbold J. (1998), "Health hazards of child labour", In : Maxcy-Rosenau-Last Public Health and Preventative medicine, Wallace R. [editor]. Stamford, CT, Appleton & Lange : pp. 697-698.

13. Lemen R.A., Layne L.A., Castillo D.N., Lancashire J.H. (1993), "Children at work : prevention of occupational injury and disease", American Journal of Industrial Medicine. 24 : 325-330.

14. Madhok, A. (1996), "Child Labour : Some Issues Some Suggestions" *Yojana,* May 1996, pp. 27-28, 42.

15. Mahapatra, S. (1997), "Steps to Check Child Labour", *Yojana,* July 1997, pp. 24-25.

16. Maskus K. (1997), "Should core labour standards be imposed

through international trade policy?" World Bank Development Research Group, Policy Research Working Paper 1817. Washington DC : The World Bank.

17. Parker, D. (1997), "Health effects of child labour," Lancet 350 : 1395-1396.
18. Pattanaik, S.N. and Daljit Singh Bedi (1998), The Menance of Child Labour—Need for an Integrated Approach", Kurukshetra, July 1998, pp. 43-48.
19. Postol, T. (1993), "Public Health and Working Children in Twentieth-Century America : An Historical Overview", Journal of Public Health Policy. Autumn : 348-354.
20. Scanlon, T. (1998), "Child Labour", [Letter] Lancet 351 : 219-220.
21. Singh, S.P. (1997), "Child Labour : The Malady and the Remedy", *Yojana,* July 1997, pp. 21-23, 27.
22. Sinha, S. (2000), "Child Labour", Kurukshetra, June 2000, pp. 29-34.
23. UNICEF (1997), "The State of the World's Children 1997", Oxford and New York : Oxford University Press for UNICEF.
24. U.S. Department of Labour (1994), "By the sweat and toil of children—Volume I : The use of child labour in American imports"—A report to the Committee on Appropriations of the U.S. Congress by the Bureau of International Labour Affairs, U.S. Department of Labour.
25. U.S. Department of Labour (1995), "By the sweat and toil of children—Volume II : The use of child labour in U.S. agricultural imports & forced and bonded child labour"—A report to the Committee on Appropriations of the U.S. Congress by the Bureau of International Labour Affairs, U.S. Department of Labour.
26. U.S. Department of Labour (1996), "Forced Labour : The Prostitution of Children", Papers from a symposium co-sponsored by the U.S. Department of Labour, Bureau of International Affairs, the Women's Bureau, and the U.S. department of State, Bureau of Democracy, Human Rights and Labour, held on September 29, 1995 at the U.S. Department of Labour in Washington DC.

16

Rehabilitation of Child Labourers—A Challenge
(A Case-Study of Child Labour Project, Kalahandi)

—*G. Rajgopal Rao**
—*Dr. R.N. Misra***

INTRODUCTION

The child population in India (*i.e.* less than 14 years of age) was nearly one-third of the total population of the country by the end of 1998. By that date the total children in Orissa constitute 12.2 million as against the total population of 36 million. Here too their number is more or less equals to one-third. In Orissa their enrolment in primary schools is just 81 per cent and the drop outs are about 46 per cent. In tribal area the drop out rate is as high as 72 per cent. Among them 51 per cent constitute girls. The official records say that the number of nor enrolment in schools is about 8,50,000. The surveys made by of different bodies constituted by Government and other private agencies state that the non-going school children (including the drop outs) are actively engaged in both hazardous and non-hazardous occupations. The reasons are obvious. Poverty is main reason. More than 60 per cent population live below poverty line (BPL). They do not get a square meal a day. Thus the gravity of the problem of child labour in India and Orissa can very well be imagined.

*Sri Rao is working as a Reader in Government Autonomous College, Bhawanipatna.

**While Dr. Misra is working as a Reader in Commerce, Science College, Hinjilicut.

OBJECTIVES AND SCOPE OF THE STUDY

The present study is made with a view to finding the real problem of child labour of Orissa in general and Kalahandi in particular. Further, it also aims to study the various rehabilitation measures taken up by both the Government and non-govt. Organisations. The scope of this study is confined to the district of Kalahandi in Orissa. In addition, the relevant data of Orissa and India have also been used for comparison.

METHODOLOGY ADOPTED FOR ANALYSES

For the purpose of the study, both primary as well as secondary data have been used. The first hand data is collected from 200 rehabilitated children of both the sexes in the district with the help of a suitably prepared questionnaire. In addition, the opinions of the rehabilitating agencies were also taken into consideration. The secondary data has been collected from various magazines, news papers, seminars, and the annual reports of certain NGOs engaged in rehabilitation of child labour in addition to their main objectives. For the purpose of analysis, ratios, percentages have been used extensively.

ABOUT ORISSA

Orissa is an Indian state of eastern region. It has a long coast line of 480 Km. It is rich with a variety of abundant natural and mineral resources. The coastal districts are affected regularly by natural calamities while the western Orissa is a drought-prone area. It has a total of 30 districts divided into 314 blocks inhabited by 86 per cent rural and 14 per cent urban/semi-urban population. About 60 per cent of its population is under BPL category. The overall literacy rate is 69 per cent while male literacy is 75 per cent and female literacy rate is 55 per cent.

The child population of the state is about 12.2 million as against the total population of 36.1 million. Due to poverty many a child is engaged in various types of hazardous and non-hazardous sectors.

ABOUT KALAHANDI

Kalahandi is an accepted Backward district of Western Orissa.

It is one of the districts of KBK region (Koraput, Bolangir and Kalahandi). The district comes a total of 22699 sq. km. area. Covering 6119 villages. The rainfall is uneven and erratic as such severe drought has become regular feature. 56% of its population comprise S.C. and S.T. Accordingly 90% of population is under BPL category. The forest coverage is 3853 km^2 which comes around 42% of total area of the district. There are no large industries. However, Kesinga, a rail head is developing as an industrial estate. In addition, 419 small-scale industries have been registered of them 200 are sick.

The child population the district too is around one third of its total population. Most of the children of both sex were engaged in some economic activity. According to an estimate of an NGO of the district there are about 85000 child labours of both the sexes, of which boys constitute 46000 while the 39000 are girls. Some of the child labour were forced by parents to work while very few (who are explain) have stated on their own accord for survival. Most of the boys were engaged in hazardous as well as non-hazardous sector.

The following table 16.1 given of gender-wise classification of child labour activity of the district.

THE PROCESS OF REHABILITATION OF CHILD LABOUR IN INDIA

The General Assembly of United Nations held : Nov., 1989, a has adopted the Child rights which fall into four basic sets like :

- The right to survival
- The right to protect
- The right to Development
- The right to participation

Perhaps in Orissa context, the first 3 sets are of paramount importance, which are inter-linked with one another.

The Govt. of India prior to U.N. Resolution in 1989, realised that mere legislation will not help in eradicating child labour. With a view to rehabilitation and reducing the number of child labour, it has adopted National Policy for Children (NPC) in 1974. The Policy states "It shall be the policy of the

Table 16.1

Male Child Labour (Boys)	*Female Child Labour (Girls)*
1. Working-gem-an-quarries	1. Sweeping & cleaning the house.
2. Stone-cutting	2. Working utensils & clothes.
3. Welding shops	3. Cooking or helping her mother-cooking.
4. Title making	4. Fetching water.
5. Brick Kilns	5. Collecting fodder and feeding animals.
6. Small hotels a sweeper/ server	6. Domestic labour in urban slums.
7. Tea stalls	7. Collecting cow dung and preparing cakes.
8. Stiching buttons in tailoring shop	8. Grazing cattle and goats, sheep.
9. Caring luggage as a porter	9. Running errand.
10. As shepards go-threads	10. Sibling care.
11. Collecting fodder and feeding the animals	11. Weaving baskets.
	12. Short term bondage to pay off loan etc.

Source : The Hindu, "Young child supplement", p. 1 dtd. 13.12.2003.

state to provide adequate nourishment to children with before and after birth and through out the period of their growth, to ensure their full physical, mental and social development" (NPC-1979). To create greater awareness and promote welfare of children including working children, a National Childrens Board was established in 1975.

The Govt. of India appointed Gurupadaswami Committee on Child Labour in 1979. The Committee emphasised on all-round development of the child including education, health and employment in industries. The Committee had also made a clear-cut distinction between Child Labour and exploitation of Child Labour. The Child Labour (Prohibition and Protection)

Act, 1986, was enacted basing on Gurupadaswami Committee Report and the recommendations of Child Labour Study Groups. The idea was to rationalise earlier legislations on Child Labour progressive elimination of Child Labour in hazardous industries and regulating the conditions of Child Labour in non-hazardous industries.

With a view to withdrawing children from hazardous work and prevent them from entering into Labour market again, the Government has implemented several schemes. The National Policy on Child Labour was adopted in 1987 which is a significant step in this regard. The future course of action, as laid down in the National Child Labour Project (N.C.L.P.) focus on the general development projects for the benefit of the existing child labour and Project plans where the concentration of Child Labour is acute.

The Hon'ble Supreme Court of India has given a clear-cut guideline in its landmark judgment on 10th Oct, 1996 in this regard. The guidelines are :

"The manner in which the engaged in hazardous sectors as defined in Child Labour Act, 1986, are to withdraw from such occupation and be rehabilitated". In non-hazardous sector, the Supreme Court has given a direction to regulate and improve the working environment of the Child Labour.

It has made education compulsory to all children in age group of (6-14). The offending employer has to pay Rs. 20,000/- per child as compensation in violation of Child Labour Act, 1986. This amount together with a matching grant of Rs. 5000/- by the State concerned be deposited in C.L. Rehabilitation-cum-Welfare Fund. The income of which should be utilized exclusively for the child concerned.

ERADICANT OF CL

Responding positively to the measures announced by Govt. of India and guidelines of Supreme Court, Orissa has set up NCLP to withdraw child labour from occupations and to rehabilitate them, so that they too can grow alongwith other previleged children of the society. At present 18 Projects of

NCLP are working in 18 districts of Orissa which are shown in Table 16.2.

Table 16.2. Zone Wise Classification of Districts Under NCLP Project of Orissa

Zones	*No. of Projects N.C.L.P.*	*Name of Districts*
North	01	Mayurbhanj at Rairangpur
West	08	Bolangir, Bargarh, Deogarh, Jharsuguda, Kalahandi, Naupada, Sambalpur, Bhawanipatna
East	02	Cuttack-Balasore
South	06	Gajapati, Ganjam, Koraput, Malkangiri, Nowrangpur, Rayagada
Central	01	Anugul
Total	18	

Source : Records of N.C.L.P., Kalahandi, Bhawanipatna.

Out of 18 districts a maximum of 8 NCLP are functioning in 8 districts of Western Zone, Orissa—followed by South Zone 6 Projects in 6 districts. North and Central zone have one NCLP each. In a recent move, the Govt. of Orissa has decided to cover all the 30 districts by establishing 12 more NCLP in the remaining 12 districts of the state.

N.C.L.P. IN KALAHANDI

N.C.L.P. in the district is functioning under the Ministry of Labour, Govt. of India. Its head office is at Naktiguda 1 K.M. away from the dist. Head Quarters Bhawanipatna. Under this a Child Labour Project Society (CLPS), Kalahandi was formed on 11.09.1995 to help rehabilitate and eradicate Child Labour gradually. It is performing its activities through various NGOs in the districts. At present there are 31 NGOs functioning in the entire district providing all sorts of help to NCLP.

The N.C.L.P. with the help of the local B.D.O., CDPO and local NGOs, conducting regular surveys in identifying the Child Labour in withdrawing them from such activities. Such

Children are admitted into special schools run by the NGOs with the support of NCLP and district administration. The NGOs concerned recruit two educational instructors, One Vocational instructor, One clerk-cum-accountant and a Peon-cum-cook—per school. All these staff are recruited locally to prevent absenteeism.

As on 31.03.2002, there are 34 NGOs actively participating in rehabilitation of Child Labour in the entire district having one municipality, 2 NACs and 13 Blocks. These NGOs since 1996, have set up 50 special schools in which the child Labour are admitted. Each school has a maximum strength of 50 children of both the sex. Thus there are 2500 child labour who have been rehabilitated so far.

Everybody each child is given a mid-day meal. In addition, each one is provided with the basic necessity like cloth, food. As most of them overaged, they have to undergo a formal education of five classes in 3 years.

Basing on the age of the child, the admission is made in first, 2nd and 3rd stage. Every child is given with a stipend of Rs. 100/- p.m. This amount is deposited in a Post Office or nearby Bank in the joint names of the child and his/her mother. The blockwise number of Schools operating by NGOs are reflected in Table 16.3.

The students, as revealed by the concerned instructors, are overaged and mature enough. They are between the age group of 8 to 12. As such, in three years they are in a position cover five years curricular as prescribed by State Govt. In the first year text books of Class-I & II are supplied. In the 2nd year text books of Class-III & IV are supplied. In the final year only text books of Class-V are supplied. After successful completion of Class-V, they are admitted into Stage Govt. run high school in Class-VI. The Annual Examination at the end of each year are managed by S.I. of Schools of the area—with centrally prepared questions and central valuation. In addition, these schools are giving more importance on extra curricular activities for 2 hours a day.

As there are special schools, the instructors should be specially trained. Within two years from Sept' 1999 to Sept'

Table 16.3. Block-Wise NGO's Run Child Labour Schools in Kalahandi

Sl. No.	*Block Name*	*No. of Schools*	*No. of NGO's running the Schools*
1.	Bhawanipatna Municipality	5	4
2.	Bhawanipatna Block	3	3
3.	Junagarh NAC	2	1
4.	Junagarah Block	3	1
5.	Kesinga NAC	2	2
6.	Kesinga Block	2	
7.	Narla Block	3	3
8.	M. Rampur	4	2
9.	Lanjigarh	3	2
10.	Karlamunda	2	2
11.	TH. Rampur	5	2
12.	Koksara	3	3
13.	Jaipatna	3	2
14.	Golamunda	3	2
15.	Dharmagarh	4	2
16.	Kalampur	3	3
	Total	50	24

Source : Records of NCLP, Kalahandi, Bhawanipatna details of all the schools and NGOs are given at the end.

01, a total of 18 training camps were arranged by the DIET. During 2002, one residential training camp was also organised for 26 instructors.

As per the records, a total of 3847 child labours of both see have so far been completed their primary education in these school upto class five. All of them have been admitted into Class-VI of high schools run by State Government since 1998-99. In 1998-99, 660 child labours were admitted into high schools. In 1999-2000 this figure rose upto 875 (35% increases). The figure declined to 369 in 2000-01. Again it has increased to 927 (about 151% increase). This figure further rose upto 1016 (about 10% increase over the preceding year).

As per the directives of Govt. of India Ministry of Labour, all the children of child labour schools are covered under Accidental Insurance Scheme for a nominal premium of Rs. 118/- for 50 student (*i.e.* Rs. 2/- per child+ service tax of Rs. 18/-). All the 2500 children of the 50 such special schools in the district have been covered under the accidental Insurance Scheme.

To prevent the children to go back to the labour market again, adequate steps and care are being exercised at every stage by these school authorities. The minds of these children are brain washed through different stories, showing motion pictures etc.

The parents of such children are also made aware of the evil effect of Child Labour. Further, they are made to realise the benefits of having Primary Education to their off springs. Now most of the parents have realised the effect of child labour and have decided not to send their children again to the labour market. Their awareness help a lot to prevent, instead of curing, child labour.

THE CHILD LABOUR SCHOOLS IN JUNAGARH

Junagarh is just 25 kms away from the Bhawanipatna, the district Head Quarter of Kalahandi (Orissa). It has one NAC and one Block. In this area two NGOs namely "Manab Seva Sanstha" (MSS) and "KARTABYA" are actively engaged in running special schools alongwith their other main activities. The former NGO runs two schools under Junagarh NAC. They are : (1) Madhusudan Child Labour and (2) Lankeswari Child Labours. The latter NGO runs three schools under Junagarh Block namely : *(i)* Dhruba Child Labour School, *(ii)* Aurobindo Child Labour School & *(iii)* Sreema Child Labour School.

These two NGOs are strictly following and implementing the Govt. of India scheme of rehabilitation of CLs. From among them CLs the SC/ST children are admitted to residential schools (for boys) and Kanyashram (for girls) which are run by Government.

The children of these schools read 5 classes in 3 years. Most of them are overaged by the time they are withdrawn from Labour market. As such there is no difficulty for them to cover class -I & II in the first year, Class-III & IV in the second year and Class-V in the third and final year. The results, as per record are wonderful. The drop outs from these school is nil, success rate is 98 per cent. After completion of 3 years, the SC/ST boys are admitted into the Govt. run residential schools, the SC/ST girls are admitted in the Kanyashrams. The other categories of children are admitted into various state run schools in the area or nearby.

One girl student, Kumari Kabita Mahakud by name, was a child labour. She was withdrawn from her work and admitted in one of these school. After completion of Class-V she was admitted in Jawahar Navodaya Vidyalaya. When she was in Class-X she was given a National Award for her courage and determination to continue her studies after being released from child labour. It is a great achievement of NCLP Kalahandi. Her determination will definitely become an ideal for other child labourers.

These schools, after completion of 3 years shift to another remote area where child labour is acute. Thus these schools are mobile in nature.

To create awareness among the general public and the parents in particular, there NGOs, which the involvement of BDOs C.D.P.Os (Child Development Project Officer) are trying their best to create a conducive environment. Appeals from collectors and Dist. Magistrate, in the form of phamplets, wall posters, are distributed. Further, the Anganwadi workers of the area are engaged in organising Literacy Campaign and meetings to explain the evils of Child Labour for the future. Even door the door campaign is also being made by these Anganwadi workers in preventing parents to send their children to labour market. In addition, street plays, songs, dramas are also organised to make the people aware of the problem. Several dignatories of central team, Secretaries, Planning Commission deputy adviser and other Law visited these schools and appreciated the way the schools are implementing the scheme of rehabilitating CLs.

The children of CLs have prepared vocational materials and opened a stall at Kalahandi Utsav usually held during Makara Sankranti period. These children too got prizes at sports meet organised by the state Govt. during 1999 and 2000 of which one got first prize and two got second prize.

OPINIONS OF THE CHILDREN OF NCLP SCHOOLS OF JUNAGARH

Of these 5 schools, 200 children were selected at random with 50% boys and 50% girls. The interaction with there has revealed the following facts.

Among 100 boys prior to their admission in these schools were working in Gem Factory, Cycle marts, Hotels, Bus-stand as Porters due to acute poverty, 82 of them were forced by their parents, 13 of them exploited by contractors and the remaining 5 are orphans who had no other go to survive.

Among the 100 girls most of them were engaged either in domestic sector and a few in hotels for washing utensils and sweeping and cleaning the floors. These girls were also forced by their parents for the same obvious reason of poverty.

When these children were withdrawn from Labour market, there was a strong protection from the parents. The NGO were patient enough in making the parents realise the evil effect of child labour and the benefit of education. Gradually parents have realised the good work of the NGOs.

The children of these school say unanimously that they would like to continue their education further and follow the example of Kabita Mahakud. They also expressed their happiness of the moment when they have participated at the Republic Day function in 1989 in a "GHUMURA TROUPE which has been telecast. They were happy to see themselves in the small screen. The Govt. of India has asked other NCLP in the country to follow the Kalahandi NCLP as an ideal.

Thus the NCLP, Kalahandi is playing a crucial and important yet challenging role in eradicating, preventing Child Labour.

List of Child Labour Schools in Kalahandi District

Sl. No.	*Name of the block municipality/NAC*	*Name of the school and location*	*Name of the N.G.O. running the school & postal address*
1	*2*	*3*	*4*
1.	Bhawanipatna Municipality	Ekalabya Child Labour School Tarini Mandir Pada, Bhawanipatna	FARR At/P.O. Bhawanipatna, Dist. Kalahandi
2.	-do-	Kasturba Child Labour School Mandar Bagicha Para, Bhawanipatna	Matrushree Mahila Mandal At/P.O. Bhawanipatna, Dist. Kalahandi
3.	-do-	Sabari Child Labour School Ramsagar Pada, Bhawanipatna	Janakalyan Snastha At/PO Bhawanipatna, Dist . Kalahandi
4.	-do-	Dharmapada Child Labour School Mahabir Pada, Bhawanipatna	Mahabir Sanskrutik Anusthan At/P.O. Bhawanipatna, Dist. Kalahandi
5.	-do-	Mahabir Child Labour School Puruna Pada, Bhawanipatna	-do-
6.	Bhawanipatna Block	Netajee Child Labour School Sapsilet (Senpur G.P.)	Netajee Yubak Sangh At/P.O. Borbhatta, Via Borda Dist. Kalahandi
7.	-do-	Sudama Child Labour School Pokharighat (Chancher G.P.)	Janakalyan Sanstha At/P.O. Bhawanipatna, Dist. Kalahandi.

(Contd.)

(Contd.)

1	2	3	4
8.	-do-	Bapujee Child Labour School Biliekuni (Kalam G.P.)	Mukti Asha Club At/P.O. Kalam, Via-Nandol, Dist Kalahandi
9.	Junagarh NAC	Madhusudan Child Labour School Junagarh (Near College)	Manab Seva Sanstha At/P.O. Junagarh, Dist. Kalahandi
10.	-do-	Lankeswari Child Labour School Junagarh (Near Hati River Check Gate)	-do-
11.	Junagarh Block	Dhruba Child Labour School Kaliakundal (Kaliakundal G.P.)	Karrtabya At/P.O. Chhoriagarh, via-Mahichala Dist. Kalahandi
12.	-do-	Aurobindo Child Labour School Banijora (Banijora G.P.)	-do-
13.	-do-	Sreema Child Labour School Borguda (Dedarah G.P.)	-do-
14.	Kesinga NAC	Gopabandhu Child Labour School Kesinga (Near College)	Brundaban Sanskrutik Anusthan At/P.O. Kesinga, Dist. Kalahandi
15.	-do-	Nachiketa Child Labour School Jolko (Kesinga)	-do-
16.	Kesinga Block	Mahatma Gandhi Child Labour School Kasrupada (Kasrupada G.P.)	-do-

(Contd.)

(Contd.)

1	*2*	*3*	*4*
17	Kesinga Block	Neelamadhab Child Labour about School Fatakamal (Patakamal G.P.)	Neelamadhab Sanskrutik Anusthan At- Pipalvadi, P.O. Pastikudi Dist. Kalahandi
18.	Narla Block	Adarsha Child Labour School Tuting (Muskuti G.P.)	Adarsha Yubak Sangh At/P.O. Rupra, Dist. Kalahandi
19.	-do-	Shravan Child Labur School Ghantmal (Ghantmal G.P.)	Jeevandhara Womens Community Trust At/P.O. Narala Road Dist. Kalahandi
20.	-do-	Gopabandhu Child Labour School Sanchishing (Santpur G.P.)	Santpur Yubak Sangh At/P.O. Santpur, Dist. Kalhandi
21.	M. Rampur Block	Ekalabya Child Labour School Mohangiri (Mohangiri G.P.)	FARR At/P.O. Bhawanipatna, Dist. Kalahandi
22.	-do-	Ekalabya Child Labour School Burat (M. Rampur G.P.)	-do-
23.	-do-	Ekalabya Child Labour School Sansurda (Gochhadengen G.P.)	-do-
24.	-do-	Rindo Majhi Child Labour School Khaliamunda (Urladani G.P.)	SEBA JAGAT At Rangapadar, P.O. Urladani Via- M. Rampur, Dist. Kalahandi

(Contd.)

(Contd.)

1	*2*	*3*	*4*
25.	Lanjigarh Block	Ekalabya Child Labour School Lanjigarh (Lanjigarh G.P.)	FARR At/P.O. Bhawanipatna, Dist. Kalahandi
26.	-do-	Ekalabya Child Labour School Bandhpari (Bandhpari G.P.)	-do-
27.	-do-	Lal Bahadur Child Labour School Padpanga (Gundri G.P.)	DAPTA At/P.O. Bhawanipatna
28.	Karlamunda Block	Kasturba Child Labour School Brahmanimunda (Risida G.P.)	Swami Vivekananda Youth Club At/P.O. Pourkela, Dist. Kalahandi
29.	-do-	Labakusa Child Labour School Karlamunda (Karlamunda G.P.)	Indira Priyadrasini Yubak Sangh At-Takarumal, P.O. Rinja, Via- Risida, Dist. Kalahandi
30.	Th. Rampur Block	Shravan Kumar Child Labour School Gunpur (Gunpur G.P.)	PARIVARTAN At/P.O. Bhawanipatna, Dist. Kalahandi
31.	-do-	Prahallad Child Labour School Vejiguda (Karlapat G.P.)	-do-
32.	-do-	Maa Manikswari Child Labour School Teba Mahul (Kaniguma G.P.)	-do-
33.	-do-	Swami Vivekananda Child Labour School Amthaguda (Karlapat G.P.)	-do-

(Contd.)

(Contd.)

1	*2*	*3*	*4*
34.	-do-	Nagavali Child Labour School Mohangiri (Nakrundi G.P)	ANTODAYA At/P.O. Kaniguma Via-Th. Rampur, Dist. Kalahandi
35.	Koksara Block	Maa Mangala Child Labour School Kulerguda (Gotomunda G.P.)	SEWA At/P.O. Gotomunda, Via-Paria, Dist. Kalahandi
36.	-do-	Budharaja Child Labour School Sagarpada (Siuni G.P)	Bhudharaja Naba Yuba Sansad At/P.O. Ampani, Dist. Kalahandi
37.	-do-	Kapileswar Child Labour School Kendudungi (Baradanga G.P.)	SANKALPA At/P.O. Laudagon, Dist. Kalahandi
38.	Jaipatna Block	Jayashree Child Labour School Mukhiguda (Mukhiguda G.P.)	Udiyaman Yubak Sangh At/P.O. Baner, Dist. Kalahandi
39.	-do-	Jai Jagannath Child Labour School Bhainripali (Bhainripali G.P.)	-do-
40.	-do-	Jayadev Child Labour School Uchhala (Uchhala G.P.)	Indira Yuba Anusthan At/P.O. Badpujhariguda, Dist. Kalahandi
41.	Golamunda Block	Sudam Child Labour School Manjheri (Manjheri G.P.)	ASRAYA At/P.O. Golamunda, Dist. Kalahandi
42.	-do-	Kegaon Child Labour School Nuagaon (Nuagaon G.P.)	Panchasakha Yubak Sangh At/P.O. Kegaon, Dist. Kalahandi

(Contd.)

(Contd.)

1	2	3	4
43.	-do-	Kapileswar Child Labour School Dhamanpur (Dhamanpur G.P.)	-do-
44.	Dharamgarh Block	Gopabandhu Child Labour School Bad Basul (Bad Basul G.P.)	GRAMODAYA At/P.O. Dharamgarh, Dist. Kalahandi
45.	-do-	Dharmapada Child Labour School Gadiajore (Gadiajore G.P.)	-do-
46.	-do-	Ahalya Child Labour School Dharamgarh (Dharamgarh G.P.)	Sarvodaya Samiti At/P.O. Dharamgarh, Dist. Kalahandi
47.	-do-	Bajirout Child Labour School Sinapada, (Parla G.P.)	-do-
48.	Kalampur Block	Ekalabya Child Labour School Gumabahal (Pandigaon G.P.)	Gopinath Club At/P.O. Pandigoan, Dist. Kalahandi
49.	-do-	Upamanyu Child Labour School Bijmara (Bijmara G.P.)	Udivaman Yubak Sangha At/P.O. Baner, Dist . Kalahandi
50.	-do-	Ambedkar Child Labour School Dhanpur (Minguru G.P.)	Dr. B.R. Amebdkar Club At/P.O. Mandal, Dist. Kalahandi

REFERENCES

1. Raj Singh Dr. Om, Child Labour Eradication, *Yojana*, Vol. 47, Nov'03 No. 11, pp. 32-37.
2. Prasad Dr. Nanda, Living it upto Enlightment, Meena, 1998, pp. 6-7.
3. Ghosh Sandeep, The future is mine, Meena, 1998, pp. 9-10.
4. Chitta R. Samant, Right to Participation, Meena, 1998, pp. 13-14.
5. – –, Children have rights too-Hi, I am Meena, p. 2, A Times of India and UNICEF Orissa, Initiation on child rights, 1998.
6. – –, Let's celebrate life, A Times of India and UNICEF Orissa, Initiation on child right, 1998, pp. 4.
7. Ramachandran Vimala, Give them their dreams, The Hindu—Young Child Quest, Dt. 13.12.03, pp. 1.
8. – –, Annual Reports of KARTABYA for 1999-2000, 2000-1, 2000-02, 2001-02.
9. – –, Detailed information on working of Child Labour Project in Kalahandi District, NCLP, Kalahandi.
10. – –, Oriya daily 'Samaj' dtd. 17.12.03.
11. – –, Meeta Meena, A Times of India and UNICEF Orissa, Initiation on Child Rights, 1998, p. 11.
12. – –, Seminar Papers on Child Labour in Hazardous Industry, Organized by Commerce & Economics Society of Orissa, in the year 2000.

Index